SEVEN PERCENT SLOWER

A Simple Trick for
MOVING PAST ANXIETY AND STRESS

By Drew Linsalata

Seven Percent Slower: A Simple Trick for MOVING PAST ANXIETY AND STRESS

ISBN: 978-1-7346164-6-0

Cover design by Zeljka Kojic

Edited by Hilary Jastram

Bookmark
PUBLISHING HOUSE

Thank You

I would like to take a moment to thank you. All of you.

Listeners of my podcast.

Readers of my books.

Members of my social media community.

Those of you who I have the honor and privilege to work with directly.

You are the fuel that drives the creation of this book. *Seven Percent Slower* was born years ago during my anxiety recovery work, but it had not seen daylight since maybe 2009. My interaction with people like you allows ideas to surface and sometimes re-surface. While ideas are wonderful, you get the credit for giving them strength, and helping them grow, and find practical application.

I appreciate you more than I can say, and I thank you from the bottom of my heart for being such an important part of this project, even if you didn't know that you were.

Resources

My Website

https://theanxioustruth.com

My Social Media Links

https://theanxioustruth.com/links

My First Two Books

https://theanxioustruth.com/recoveryguide

https://theanxioustruth.com/mystory

My Podcast

https://theanxioustruth.com/listen

Table of Contents

Table of Contents

Foreword

Hello, and a warm and sincere well done for picking up this book. I know that reading any content relating to your fears can be challenging, but rest assured, this book is a safe space for you to be you. As a psychotherapist who specializes in working with anxiety disorders, let me assure you that this excellent book can be an invaluable tool in recovery from disordered anxiety. I am someone who was crippled by anxiety for many years, and refreshingly, I recognize that Drew has outlined some of the elements of my own recovery that I have previously failed to put into words.

For many years I believed that my anxious feelings were something I needed to rapidly fix. Like many others with disordered anxiety, I am an intelligent problem-solver; I simply want to get stuff done, so I can move on and get on with more life tasks. I, like many others with disordered anxiety, am also good at getting stuff done. So, it came as a huge surprise when these scary feelings of doom, unease, and fear struck me from seemingly nowhere and didn't seem to go away. I developed excessive fear, then a fear of this excessive fear. I began to fear panic, which inevitably became a problem that I wanted to fix and get done! I didn't like this at all, nor did the part of me that wanted to hastily remove annoying obstacles in my life. Inevitably, I made overcoming anxiety a "task" that I wanted to rush through, which—as you're probably familiar with—does not work.

Back in the midst of my anxiety disorder, I didn't have the resources available today to help me learn about my condition.

I just thought I had lost my mind, and I would be forever trapped in a purgatory of fear. I thought I'd be spending every day for the rest of my life being hypervigilant of anxiety and its many symptoms and sensations. However, learning about excessive, disordered anxiety, including the biomechanics, the science, and the psychology, led me to begin to trial and error my way out of its clutches. My road to recovery was not simple, nor was it linear, but thankfully the information available from the right people today can help your recovery go along more smoothly. Drew Linsalata is a fantastic educator on the topic of anxiety disorders, and his teachings are a wonderful asset to anyone recovering.

Why is it important to slow down during recovery from an anxiety disorder? An important aspect of my own recovery was learning not to rush through things. I had to postpone that often useful part of me that wanted to complete everything as fast as I could. As you may or may not know by now, exposure to your fears is essential when tackling certain presentations of anxiety, including panic disorder, agoraphobia, social anxiety, driving anxiety, flying anxiety, etc. This doesn't mean we have to jump in at the deep end, but it does mean that we have to dip our toe in the water to test it out. We must begin to lean toward our fears in the knowledge that anxiety and its many symptoms are safe to experience and cannot hurt us. This was a daunting prospect for someone who struggled to even leave his room for six months, but I'm here today and proud of what I achieved; I am now one of the leading voices on anxiety disorders in the UK.

One of my golden rules when working with clients is to "do what non-anxious you would do, despite being anxious." When we are experiencing fear, and our fight-or-flight response is engaged, it can feel instinctual to want to run away or venture toward a place of "safety." This is okay to feel this—it is normal. Drew and I have felt this many a time. However, part of recovery is to ignore this fear response in times when we don't need it. Part of recovery for me was to continue to do what non-anxious me would do. I would ask myself, "Would non-anxious me want to rush through this exposure?" "Would non-anxious me be desperately foraging for a bottle of water or some safety object/place/person right now?" Learning to slow down to a pace that my non-anxious self would operate at was so important in my recovery.

Ultimately, recovering from excessive anxiety is when we turn the brain's threat response off in situations where we don't need it—usually normal, everyday situations. We do this by showing the threat response that this situation we want to feel "normal" in is not dangerous. This means resisting the urge to rush, to be frantic, to count down the seconds until we can escape, or to step hastily toward where we feel we may be less anxious. With panic disorder and agoraphobia, the threat response learns from our behavior and decides whether or not to trigger in the future—dependent on our behaviors. If it remembers that you rushed, ran away, "white-knuckled," or sought immediate reassurance in a situation from your recent past, it will trigger anxiety again and again. It won't necessarily get worse, but it can often leave us in a place where we feel stuck.

Drew's suggestion of taking things Seven Percent Slower is perfect. It's a concept taken from the abstract and a helpful reminder that we don't need to fervently writhe in our scary exposures, but we can learn to take a breath and lean toward what our non-anxious selves would do. This is where the magic happens.

I spent many months hitting roadblocks with my exposures because I didn't necessarily have the correct guidance or the right information. This was partly down to rushing through scary situations or hoping that merely putting myself in a scary situation was enough to "fix" me. I did the hard part, which was being brave enough to try exposure, but accepting the feelings and taking things at a slower pace during these challenging times was absolutely key for both me and my brain to realize that I could cope in these situations. This is recovery. This is what we try to educate people about.

There's a lot of information and misinformation about anxiety out there. I spend a lot of my time discerning what is helpful from what is not, particularly in regard to anxiety disorders. I would like to personally and publicly thank Drew for his invaluable insights, which have grown from both his research and his often relatable, personal phenomenology. His experiences have clearly shaped his passion for his work, but his empathy stands out above all else. It is due to this that I give this book my coveted seal of approval.

Enjoy.

Joshua Fletcher

IG, Facebook, Twitter: @anxietyjosh

Author of *Anxiety: Practical About Panic*

Introduction

Why Seven Percent Slower?

I used to be an anxious, frightened mess.

It's true. I struggled on and off for many years of my life with crippling anxiety disorders and depression.

I am living proof that anxiety disorders and depression are not life sentences. After struggling for 25-plus years with panic attacks, agoraphobia, intrusive thoughts, obsessions and compulsions, and crippling depression, I learned how to handle those problems myself.

I didn't use magic herbs, crystals, tapping techniques, or motivational quotes. I solved my mental health problems using tried-and-true science-based cognitive behavioral tools that drove me directly INTO what I feared and avoided the most. I got better with knowledge, hard work, tenacity, persistence, and patience.

I educated myself.

I made it my job to learn the theory and mechanics of anxiety and anxiety disorders and apply them to my situation.

In doing so, I stopped seeing anxiety and fear as my enemies and transformed them into my teachers. I traded in a small, fear-based life for a liberating life free of anxiety-related restrictions.

Along the way, I learned about and incorporated invaluable recovery and mental health tools into my life. I trained myself to focus sharply when needed. I conditioned myself to relax my body even when my mind was far from it. I appreciated the value of living in the moment as I practiced being mindful. If there was a tool I could use to advance my recovery, I learned it and applied it. If there was no tool available to help me with a given issue, I invented one, then applied it.

This is how Seven Percent Slower, a little mental trick I used to slow myself down, was born.

When I first thought of the concept, I didn't think much of it. It was something I came up with for my use because, frankly, I REALLY needed a way to stop pouring gasoline on my raging anxiety fire. Focusing on becoming Seven Percent Slower proved to be extremely useful to me in those days. As it turns out, it has remained extremely useful to me ever since.

I will be going Seven Percent Slower when needed for the rest of my days!

Now that I spend a large percentage of my time writing, speaking, teaching, and supporting others on the topic of anxiety and anxiety recovery, Seven Percent Slower has taken on new life. I've been using it as an awareness device when supporting others as they recover from their anxiety and mental health issues. At first, I used it casually in a few conversations. In every case, the response was quite favorable. I was told that the concept was useful and easy to use. Then I mentioned Seven Percent Slower here and there on my social media channels. Again, the feedback was universally positive. Members of my social media community, anxious people trying to become non-anxious, all seem to love and use Seven Percent Slower.

After being asked to make *Seven Percent Slower* t-shirts, mugs, and hoodies (not really my jam), it finally dawned on me that what I should be doing is writing this book! So, here I am, pounding away on a keyboard in June 2021 in hopes that I can teach you how to use Seven Percent Slower as a tool to make your life less full of anxiety, fear, and stress.

I'm happy you've decided to come along for the ride.

And I can't wait to teach you the little trick that changed my life.

Who Is This Book For?

Seven Percent Slower was written for people who find themselves anxious, afraid, and stressed, and as a result, wind up racing around all day without knowing exactly why they're moving at light speed.

If you've ever found yourself tearing through the act of making a sandwich without having the slightest idea of why you're going so damn fast, then *Seven Percent Slower* is for you.

If you are anxious, afraid, or stressed out all the time, then this book is for you. If you are looking for ways to improve your anxiety situation, reduce stress, be less afraid, and drop your overall nervous energy level, then *Seven Percent Slower* will likely prove valuable to you. If you find yourself wound up like a spring most of the time, then learning how to go Seven Percent Slower should make your life at least a little better.

The principle of going Seven Percent Slower is a valuable component in anxiety recovery but can also demystify and simplify the idea of mindful living in general. If you are interested in mindfulness but get overwhelmed thinking about applying it to your life, *Seven Percent Slower* will help you become more mindful without having to try so damn hard to do it.

I would like to think that Seven Percent Slower is a concept that almost any modern human in the Western would find helpful. We all rush through our days for no good reason at times. Learning how *not to do that* could meaningfully impact your life.

Who Am I?

I am not only a former anxiety and depression sufferer; I am now a writer, speaker, and educator on the topics of anxiety and anxiety recovery. I am the creator and host of *The Anxious Truth* podcast, which helps people with anxiety issues, is now closing in on two million downloads, and has been on the air since 2014.

I am the author of two bestselling books on anxiety:

1. *An Anxiety Story: How I Recovered from Anxiety, Panic and Agoraphobia*

2. *The Anxious Truth: A Step-By-Step Guide to Understanding and Overcoming Panic, Anxiety and Agoraphobia.*

I am also fortunate to sit at the head of a large and growing social media table and help a highly engaged group of amazing humans find information, education, inspiration, and support for the anxiety and mental health problems they are struggling to overcome.

It is my honor to use my knowledge and life experiences to help others solve the mental health problems I once thought to be unsolvable. And I would not have it any other way.

Oh, and one more thing. If you find that you are rushing and trying to read this book as fast as you can, please stop and slow down. Because ... you know ... irony.

Chapter 1 — No Days Off: The Frantic Life of an Anxious Brain

Your brain REALLY needs a few days off.

Anxiety, fear, and stress will drive your brain to work harder than a one-legged man in an ass-kicking contest.

Being a human brain in charge of an anxious person is a thankless job. Every day the to-do list is long, and the pay is low. So, what does a typical day on the job look like for your anxious brain?

First come the thoughts, thoughts, thoughts, thoughts, and more thoughts. Then you can't ignore the rituals to engage in and the triggers to scan for, so you can be sure to avoid them. Next, there are the stories you have to tell yourself about how anxious you are and how horrible feeling like that is. Your brain's inbox is full of panicky, scary memories, all needing to be processed. And we've only made it as far as lunch! After lunch, your brain attends endless, soul-crushing rumination and worry meetings. Then the unfulfilled hopes and dreams reports must be done, and there's decision paralysis and self-pity to sort out before the 3 PM coffee break. To top it all off, if your brain doesn't get all your anxiety symptom checking and the comparing of how your life must suck more than anyone else's on Facebook finished before quitting time, it will have to work a double shift!

By the time your brain finishes all its work for the day and drags itself to bed, it struggles to get to sleep because, well … there's always so much to think about! Your brain tosses and turns, fumbles with the blankets, tries to find a cool spot on the pillow and gets frustrated that sleep is not coming. After enough time passes, your bleary-eyed brain runs out of gas and dozes off for a while. Then the alarm sounds in the morning, and it's time to do it all over again!

Even if you're not struggling with a serious anxiety problem, odds are your poor brain is still on a similar hamster wheel and in need of a break.

If you're anything like most people in the Western world, you are spending your days stressed, rushed, harried, frazzled, trying to keep up, and doing your best to hold it together.

You are tending to yourself, your family, your relationships, your finances, your job or business, your pets, your hobbies, and all the stuff that you always say you *want* to get around to someday, but (kind of) never do. No matter what you do, there always seems to be another goal, another task, and another issue to deal with.

It never ends.

All the while, your brain is in overdrive, keeping track of all the chainsaws and torches it is being asked to juggle. There's nothing but work to do for your brain, and it seems there's no break in sight.

Good times, right?

Well, take solace in knowing that regardless of what has your brain amped up and working overtime every damn day, you are not alone. Not by a long shot. It's safe to assume if you lined up 100 people and asked them to read the previous few paragraphs, at least 70 of them would knowingly nod as they did. Having an overworked and over-stressed brain is incredibly common in our modern world.

But … why?

Why is your brain, and the brains of so many people you know and love, working overtime? What's going on?

Let's skip the commentary on life today and its moral, ethical, and practical downfalls. That's for another book and likely another author.

Instead, let's look at how you perceive and process things. Let us examine how your brain learns to interpret the world and does its best to keep stuff running smoothly for you.

The more primitive parts of your brain are designed to do basic things that you don't need to have conscious control over. It's better that way. Imagine having to manage every breath, heartbeat, and bead of sweat. Life is already challenging enough, so nature was kind and has not forced us to handle those tasks. They are automated. Go nature!

But ... nature has also automated another important task for us: threat detection and response. Enter your amygdala. Your fear center. Your "lizard brain."

I just like the word "lizard," so I'm going to use that to refer to the part of your brain responsible for sensing threats and keeping you safe from them.

Back in "the day," humans were surrounded all the time by very real threats to their actual survival. Enemy tribes and social groups competed for resources like food and water, shelter in harsh conditions, and battling sicknesses that nobody understood because there was no medicine.

Nature is harsh.

We've spent thousands of years learning to protect ourselves from it, for the most part. But way back when we were at the mercy of nature, it was good at kicking all kinds of human and protohuman ass. (According to Oxford Languages, a protohuman is: "A hypothetical, prehistoric primate, resembling humans and thought to be their ancestor, whose profile has been compiled mostly from fossil evidence.")

It was not easy to be an early human. But nature was smart enough to give us an excellent threat detection and response system. It works all by itself and doesn't need us to do much thinking to stay safe when the sh-t hits the fan.

We are now living in very different times. The overall threat to survival for a modern human in the 21st-century Western world is FAR lower than it was 20,000 years ago. However, we must also acknowledge that this is not true for every modern human. Food and shelter insecurities are very real problems for far too many people. But for the most part, the vast majority of us are not spending our days worrying about staying alive. The threats that your lizard brain evolved to defend you against do not largely exist.

So, what does a perfectly good lizard brain—an expert at finding and responding to threats and danger—do when it finds itself with lots of free time? It finds threats and tells you to respond to them! That seems silly, but your lizard brain doesn't know how to do anything else.

Your lizard brain is spending most of its time dealing with two main jobs that it must work very hard at.

The first job is to find threats. It will scan your environment continually for threats because keeping you alive and safe is super important. It will look for threats to your physical safety and well-being. When it finds none, it will look for emotional threats, social threats, mental threats, financial threats, relation-ship and romantic threats, and anything else it can get its confused little mitts on. You do not need this most of the time, but your lizard brain does not know this, so it remains vigilant and ready to spring into action!

Allow me to clarify that last bit.

Your lizard brain isn't ready to "spring into action" per se. It is a bit too lazy for that. What it is super-hypervigilant about is instructing every other part of your body and brain, so *they* will spring into action! In many ways, your lizard brain is like the annoying kid who wants to pick fights for no reason, only to turn tail and hide behind his big brother when someone wants to throw down. It doesn't know how to run, flee, fight, avoid, or escape. Your lizard brain doesn't have arms or legs or complex processing and decision-making skills. So, when it gets busy looking for threats where none really exist, it will make some up, then light a fire under the rest of you to get YOU to take evasive action. What a jerk!

What Does Evasive Action Look and Feel Like?

Evasive action feels like fear, stress, uncertainty, feelings of impending doom or disaster, worry, rumination, and obsession. Evasive action looks like avoidance, escape, distraction, and soothing. What evasive action *really* looks like is SPEED. Evasive action, when demanded by a misguided lizard brain, is fast, rushed, and urgent. Your fear center/lizard brain decides that the churning in your stomach or your growing credit card bills are important threats to your safety. So, it pushes the panic button. Then you will obey and leap into action without any awareness that you are being ordered around by a sentry with little to stand guard for. You will, by and large, speed up.

Throughout this somewhat broken process, there are likely times when you are cognizant of how jacked up the lizard brain is. In moments of clarity, you will declare, "This is not an acceptable way to live!" You will say, "I need to do something about my anxiety," or that you must "get yourself out of the rat race," or "off the endless hamster wheel of stress." Yet somehow, those plans, as well-intentioned as they are, never seem to work out.

Why?

Your lizard brain has no ears or eyes. At least not in the way we think of them. It is aware at a primitive level. All it knows is danger or safety. It isn't aware of words, logic, reason, common sense, motivational quotes, or inspirational memes. So, when you decide that you have had enough of feeling battered by the lizard brain and you want to make a change, you naturally decide to *start to THINK* differently about your situation.

"I refuse to be stressed by this anymore!"

"I'm done playing this game!"

"Everyone can go f-ck themselves. I'm not letting them bother me."

"Obviously, these sensations are not dangerous, so I'm not going to care about them anymore!"

Logically, this makes perfect sense!

After all, "change your thoughts, change your life," right? We hear that phrase often enough. But as it turns out, this isn't the case, at least as far as that pesky lizard brain is concerned. You can think all you want and be as angry and resolved to make a change as you want to be.

Your lizard brain is not listening.

It cannot hear you.

It doesn't understand.

Furthermore, it doesn't care.

Remember when I said that nature was smart enough to give us an automatic threat detection system that doesn't need our attention or conscious intervention? Let's take that to another level.

Nature was also smart enough NOT to allow us to easily turn off that threat detection system. From an evolutionary perspective, we can imagine that early humans who had lizard brains that would shut up when told to do so likely died out. That would be bad design, wouldn't it? If all you had to do in the face of a threat was read a few Eckhart Tolle passages to turn off your flight or fight response, you would become vulnerable to real danger.

In nuclear energy plants, alert systems can't be silenced by one annoyed employee hitting a single button. It wouldn't be safe. Alert systems in that environment are designed and built to FORCE action. Engineers built systems that scream, "SOMETHING IS WRONG, AND I WILL NOT BE QUIET UNTIL YOU FIX IT OR SHOW ME OTHERWISE!" Your lizard brain—your threat detection and alert system—is wired the same way. Be angry, frustrated, and annoyed if you want, but you can't turn it off by thinking or talking at it.

In a nuclear plant, an alert MUST be responded to. Action must be taken. An investigation must be made. Multiple employees and operating systems must come together to agree there is a threat, and that action is appropriate, or that there is no threat, and the alarm can be silenced. The same holds true for you and your old buddy—your lizard brain.

You will have to act to silence the alarm or at least turn down the volume. Your lizard brain needs to be SHOWN that it can stand down. It needs to EXPERIENCE a "green light" condition before it will learn to sit down and be quiet until really needed.

What Experiences Can We Provide to Change Things?

You may be struggling with anxiety, or you may be chronically stressed. In both cases, you are looking for ways to get that damn lizard brain to chill out and take a few days off. Regardless of the specifics of your situation (anxiety or stress), you'll shut off the lizard alarm by feeding your fear center/lizard brain appropriate experiences and behavioral signals. You will SHOW it through your action that the coast is clear; you will feed it experiences in which you do not launch yourself into disaster mode yet still wind up OK. When you do this, you are teaching your lizard brain that there are other experiences to be had than reactionary panic.

This, in simple terms, is how you get your stressed, anxious, afraid, overworked brain the break it needs and deserves.

Now...

What actions can you take to accomplish this goal?

What signals can you send your trigger-happy lizard brain? How can you show it that everything is OK so that it can grab a beer and kick back for a while instead of dragging you around like an out-of-control bobblehead doll?

One action you can take would be to SLOW DOWN. Even just a little.

You know, maybe go SEVEN PERCENT SLOWER.

Hey, that seems like a good idea, doesn't it?

Chapter 2 — SPEED: A Natural Response to Anxiety, Stress, and Fear

You do it.

I do it.

We all do it.

We do it even when we don't know we're doing it.

Furthermore, we prefer not to do it.

But we do it anyway.

Then we see how much it stinks.

And we swear that we will stop doing it.

But we don't stop.

We want to, but we don't.

Am I talking about over-eating?

Drinking too much?

Speaking when we should be listening?

Making bad relationship choices?

Wearing white after Labor Day (this is an American fashion joke, and I will expect praise for making a ... FASHION JOKE!)?

Nope. I'm talking about rushing.

Speeding up.

Accelerating.

Moving through our tasks and thoughts like we are being chased by the Grim Reaper.

This is what we do accidentally, inadvertently, and repeatedly, even though in modern times it is ... by and large ... an awful coping strategy (unless you are actually being chased by the Grim Reaper—then as you were).

Before we dive into what propels us to move so quickly, let's take a moment to talk about fight, flight, and freeze.

You've probably heard about fight or flight. But lately, the "freeze" response is demanding equal time in the discussion of fear responses. Fair enough, freeze, we can acknowledge you. However, this book is mainly about fight and flight. They are the most well-studied variants of the typical threat response, and within large populations, are also the most common.

It is not my intention to dismiss or invalidate the "freezers" among us. Some people do have forms of freezing as their primary threat response style. We all have a bit of freeze in us occasionally.

What Does Freeze Look Like?

Freeze looks like "checking out." Being unable to act. Becoming passive. Freeze often involves a decrease in energy level, at least when observed from the outside. When you ask most freeze responders to slow down, they will tell you that they are not rushing because they often feel paralyzed and unable to do anything in the face of fear—much less do it quickly.

So, while I want to acknowledge our freeze comrades in the battle against anxiety, fear, and stress, I do have to be honest and say that I did not write this book for you. For the most part, you do not have the problem—fear-driven speed and rushing—that I am writing about, so you will likely find most of what I am talking about to be outside your wheelhouse.

When we are afraid, most of us tend to move through space and time like we were shot out of a cannon. We talk faster, walk faster, and think faster (although not necessarily in a productive way). We move through our days like we are trying to break a speed record for making lunch or getting from one end of the frozen foods section to the other. An anxious, stressed, afraid person is often easily identified by how fast they are going.

How many times have people told you
to "slow down and take a breath"?

Why do you think they say that to you? They can see you behaving like a cracked-out speed demon. That's why.

And mostly … you are.

Accelerating, going faster, and rushing through everything is a natural part of the escape and avoidance response to fear, anxiety, and stress. When your lizard brain goes looking for trouble and finds it, it will demand that you get yourself to safety. A key part of this strategy involves speeding you up. It looks a bit like this scenario:

Sister-in-law: "Is that a new skirt? "

You: "Yes, I just found it and had to get it. Got a good deal, too!"

Sister-in-law: "I had one like that. I wound up returning it because it made me look like a beached whale."

LIZARD BRAIN: "Uhm … did she just call you a beached whale???"

You: "I don't think so. She said…."

LIZARD BRAIN: "Beached whale! This skirt makes you look like a beached whale! You clearly have no idea how to choose clothing properly. Remember when you were annoyed at yourself for eating that second slice of pizza? This is what happens. I hope you're happy!"

You: "Do you really think she meant it that way?"

LIZARD BRAIN: "Look, who is here is to keep you out of trouble? I AM! So, trust me on this. Of course, she meant it that way. She sees your terrible life skills and your weight problem. She knows that you can't get your sh-t together no matter how hard you try. Not only that, but she sees right through you! That skirt thing was just her polite way of letting you know! How do you not see this???"

You: "OMG! What should I do?"

LIZARD BRAIN: "GET OUT OF HERE! This is nothing but a den of vipers, and you're headed for a major disaster if you let them circle you. They'll find you out, and you'll be kicked out of the family and left all alone. GET! OUT! NOW!!!!!!"

You: "OK, we'll leave right after I finish my tea."

LIZARD BRAIN: "FASTER! I NEED YOU TO FINISH THAT TEA IMMEDIATELY AND GET OUT OF HERE! GO FASTER!"

See how this played out? In this example, we looked at socially based anxiety and stress, but we could have used any stress or anxiety trigger. A twitch in your tummy that gets interpreted as disaster. A news story you overhear talking about cancer that launches you into a spiral of health worry and obsession. Anything that creates an anxiety, fear, or stress response will kick this mechanism into gear. When anxious, afraid, or stressed, one of the prime directives your lizard brain will issue to the rest of your mind and body is "GO FASTER!"

Rushing and going faster are natural and baked-in aspects of the escape and avoidance responses. They are attempts to get away from the stressor, fear trigger, or threat response. They are part of fight or flight. If you're going to run away from the perceived threat, going faster *is* an advantage. If you're going to turn and fight, being quicker and faster *are* advantages.

If you are tasked with the critically important job of staying alive in the face of real danger or your possible demise, going faster is highly desirable. Speed improves survival performance in most cases. Speed gets the job done more quickly and effectively, allowing you to live to see another day. In a world full of real, constant, actual threats to your existence as an individual and to the perpetuation of the human species, the ability to accelerate is good design. *Was a good design*. Rushing around and speeding up when stressed or afraid was likely an evolutionary imperative.

But in the 21st century in the developed world, this genius bit of evolutionary engineering has become less important, and in many cases, it causes more harm than it prevents.

Speeding up kept primitive man alive.
Speeding up keeps modern man stuck in a cycle of
threat scanning, false alarms, fear, stress, and anxiety.

Maybe one day, if we wait another million years or so, evolution will adjust this for humanity. Lizard brain version 2.0 will hopefully have a richer feature set that allows it to make better choices and read the room more skillfully before losing its sh-t and firing you up into a frenzied state.

For now, we have to work with what we've been given, so let's do that.

Chapter 3 — What Does Your Speed Response Look Like?

Rushing is a thing we often do without realizing that we're doing it.

This is why in the last chapter, I pointed out that you've likely been told to slow down by anyone observing you in speed-demon mode.

Your lizard brain is hella fast. It operates quickly enough that you can't really interact with its process until the launch sequence has been activated. So, you will find yourself rushing around and running through life before you even know it. This is standard, so don't feel bad when you discover that you are in high gear and you feel like your brain has tricked you again. We all get tricked. This is how humans work.

But once you realize it, then you can do something about it.

You are not doomed to a life of frantic activity.
You're not even doomed to a day or hour of it.

Not only that, but you can pump the behavioral and cognitive brakes and change things. You may have to repeat this exercise quite often to master it, but that's OK, too. This is what you need to do to retrain your lizard brain successfully.

But let's not get ahead of ourselves. Before you can enact any major change, it helps to recognize what your particular speed response looks like.

Often the first signs of stress/fear-based acceleration can be found in your thoughts or what you tell yourself when responding to fear, anxiety, and stress. Typical thoughts and self-talk statements can look like this:

"OMG, I hate this!"

"I need to get out of here!"

"I just want this over as quickly as possible!"

"I need to get back to my comfort zone fast!"

"My body has a mind of its own!"

"I feel trapped and have to get out NOW!"

"All I want to do is get this done, so I can relax."

"I don't have time for this now! I have so much to worry about and do!"

Do any of these thoughts or statements sound familiar to you?

When anxious, stressed, or afraid, take a quick inventory of what you think about and what you say to yourself. It might help for you to take a short break now, grab a pen and paper, and jot down the usual thoughts that pop into your anxious brain when you are feeling at the height of your anxiety. Which of these statements are demands for speed? Which will trigger the rushing around? Which thoughts focus on the future–specifically, getting through the current situation, so you can find safety, calm, or relaxation to feel better?

This little exercise of simply jotting down the thoughts that plague your anxious brain can help you identify the signs of your speed response, so you can act to interrupt that process and … oh, I don't know … slow down by some small percentage.

Let's examine some physical signs and manifestations of your speed response. When anxious, afraid, and stressed, you may engage in some or all of these habits:

- Breath holding
- Shortening your walking stride
- Increasing your walking speed
- Tensing your muscles
- Grimacing or clenching your jaw
- Darting your eyes back and forth
- Fumbling or dropping things
- Shaking
- Stumbling over your words
- Furiously "doom scrolling" your favorite social media feeds
- Engaging in the "self-hug" or hunching over in a defensive posture

Of course, these thinking and behavioral habits are not necessarily rushing behaviors by themselves. They are indicators, though. Flags. Signals you can check for. When you find yourself engaging in enough of them at the same time, there is a good chance that you are rushing around because you are afraid, anxious, or stressed to the max!

Another way you can tell that you are in escape-focused speed-demon mode is by how you manage your behaviors and thoughts.

Are you ending conversations quickly and un-naturally to get away from being trapped?

Are you leaving tasks unfinished, dropping them on the floor, and making a half-hearted promise to yourself to return and complete them when you feel better?

Are you postponing the tasks or appointments that lie ahead of you because you just want to get through the discomfort you're feeling and return to a position of safety, soothing, and increased calm?

Do you find yourself putting your head down and refusing to engage with the world around you to more quickly exit the situation you are in?

These are all valuable hints that tell you when your lizard brain has ordered your brain and body into high gear.

These behaviors all represent efforts to escape from your anxiety and fear triggers or whatever is ramping up your stress level.

The following are the cognitive and behavioral calling cards of your speed response:

- Thinking quickly but not terribly effectively with the goal of escape.

- Propelling your body through space and time so quickly that your physical function suffers.

- Terminating engagements and existing situations because you have "had enough" or feel that you can't handle it.

These are the signs telling you that you are on the fear and stress Autobahn. On this road, there is no speed limit and going as fast as possible to escape is the only goal that matters to you. Before you can learn how to go slower—maybe Seven Percent Slower—you will need to learn how to recognize your speed response and rushing habits, so you can intervene and correct your reactions.

---

*Here's your first little hack designed
to help you slow things down.*

After you take the time to jot down all your rushing and speed habits, take more time to refer to your list a few times each day. Learning to go Seven Percent Slower requires that you treat this task like studying for an exam. The more you go over your notes, the more familiar you will be with the material. Know your habits. Firmly implant them in your head. Knowing them well will help you as we go down this road.

After you've done your homework and gone over your speed habits, do your best to insert a pause somewhere in the first minute or so of your anxiety or stress response. When you feel the emotion welling up and know you're nearing the end of your fear or stress rope and want to explode, stop. Just for 30 seconds. Go back to your speed habits list. If you need a cheat sheet, keep your list on your phone to access it fast. Scan the list mentally or on your phone, then make a note to remind yourself to be on the lookout for your thinking and behavioral habits. This serves two purposes.

1. It will help you recognize when you go into high gear more quickly, so you can act to downshift (slow down) before you get carried away.

2. Paying attention to your speed habits means you are paying less attention to your anxiety and stress-fueling thoughts. Shift your job from responding to catastrophic and negative thoughts to paying attention to what you're actually doing from moment to moment. It is harder to pour fuel on your fear and stress fire when you are actively engaged in a more productive task.

If you have been listening to my podcast (theanxioustruth.com/ listen) or reading my other books (theanxioustruth.com/book-updates), you may be jumping up and down now and screaming, "But Drew! Isn't that distraction?" If you are, good job. It's the right question to ask.

Here's the difference and why moving your mind to make better decisions is not a distraction. You've heard me talk about how intent matters, and in this situation, *you are not attempting to drown out anxiety, fear, or stress. You are engaging in a productive task even while feeling stress-based or fear-based sensations and hearing fear and stress-based thoughts.*

This first little hack isn't designed to distract you. It is perfectly in alignment with our desire to learn to function productively even when we feel that we can't.

Know your speed response and rushing habits, then start working on recognizing them when they get triggered. This is your first step toward going Seven Percent Slower.

Chapter 4 — Why Rushing Around Is a Bad Idea

Automatically speeding up when anxious, afraid, or stressed was an excellent idea 20,000 years ago.

In 2021, not so much. Let's look at why.

First, it is important to recognize and understand the difference between actual danger and disordered anxiety or modern-day stress.

When confronted with an actual threat, acceleration serves a purpose! We can argue the merits of remaining "cool under pressure," of course (a valuable skill), but we truly NEED our ability to accelerate automatically. If it really is time to fight or flee, the ability to throw hands or get the hell out of Dodge faster than our opponents is a good thing.

In the face of disordered anxiety or stress exacerbated by a hyperactive lizard brain sounding false alarms, acceleration sends the wrong signal back to your brain. It makes sense then that learning to go Seven Percent Slower is all about signals.

It's damn near impossible to refuse the initial command to sound the alarm from your lizard brain. So, when we choose to keep rushing around in an effort to escape our discomfort and unease, we send an important signal. While your lizard brain is looking for the "all clear," you are telling it that the situation is anything *but clear*. By going faster and faster, you are shouting at your lizard brain that there really is a threat that needs dealing with. It will get that signal, conclude that it is still needed, and continue to fire "danger" directives at the rest of your body and brain.

Given a chance, it will happily repeat that performance.

This is why rushing around as a stress or anxiety response is a bad idea.

When your lizard brain wants you to speed up to avoid danger, but there is no danger, accelerating rewards it for being wrong!

When you rush around because you are anxious, stressed, and afraid, you are needlessly ratcheting up your energy level and your arousal level (this is uncomfortable as all get out!). You are also all but guaranteeing that your fear center will continue to trigger and encourage this behavior in the future.

When you obey the order to speed up and remain in speed-demon mode for long periods of time, you are keeping the anxiety and stress fire burning brightly. The behavior you think will get you to a better place winds up cementing you in a block of stress, fear, and discomfort.

Zooming around is a bad idea because it quite literally instructs your overworked, trigger-happy brain to keep tripping the danger alarm at the slightest sign of anything going wrong.

Engaging in human zoomies is the opposite
of calming your hyperactive threat response.
It is like feeding it a steady diet of caffeine,
sugar, and crystal meth.

Rushing around creates ... more rushing around. Speed breeds more speed. The hamster wheel of the overworked brain and its demand for speed is relentless. It will just keep spinning if you just keep running.

Let's take a moment to circle back and summarize what we've discussed so far.

1. Nestled comfortably in your brain is a fear center tasked with detecting threats and ordering you into fight or flight mode. It operates quickly and without much finesse. This is your "lizard brain." It is horribly outdated, like a Members Only jacket.

2. Your lizard brain is ideally suited for the environmental and social conditions for which it was designed over tens of thousands of years. Evolution is slow, however, so some people find their lizard brains a bit too enthusiastic. It will scan the environment for threats zealously.

3. This will lead your lizard brain to sound the alarm in many situations where discomfort and uncertainty exist, but not actual danger.

4. When your lizard brain detects danger, it will order the rest of your brain and body to speed up. Speed was needed more often to escape or survive back in the day, but in today's environment, most of the dangers our primitive ancestors dealt with do not exist, so hyperactive speed is rarely required.

5. Your lizard brain only understands experiences and behavioral signals, so when it sounds the alarm, it looks to those cues for confirmation that the danger does not exist or has passed.

6. Obeying the initial order to speed up is natural and unavoidable. When you keep taking orders from your lizard brain, you prolong the rushing and speeding up. This means you are accidentally choosing to send a continuous stream of danger signals back down the line, keeping your lizard brain in a state of high alert. This is also why you feel stressed, overwhelmed, anxious, and afraid so much of the time.

7. One way we can help to respond more productively and improve your stress, fear, and anxiety situation is to get your brain to take some time off. You'll want to get it to stand down, kick back, and stop sounding alarms all day long.

8. You can send your brain on vacation by slowing down. When you slow down, you send "all clear" signals to your lizard brain, allowing it to start its long-overdue break that it—and you—so desperately need.

9. I call the little mental trick you can use to slow down "Seven Percent Slower." That's what this book is all about!

10. There really is no number ten, but I hate lists that end at nine, so here we are.

Now that we have seen what creates the firestorm of stress, fear, anxiety, and speed, let's talk about the benefits of learning to go Seven Percent Slower. We will examine how it fits into concepts like mindfulness and being present. Finally, we will explore practical tips to use to slow you down and get you off this hamster wheel.

But first, let me address a common objection to slowing down….

Chapter 5 — "But then I'll feel things!" (Why you might not want to go slower.)

You may be thinking to yourself that you are well aware of your propensity to speed things up when afraid, anxious, or stressed.

And you may well be aware of why accelerating is a bad idea.

Furthermore, you likely truly understand how involuntary racing around makes sense from a pure fight or flight perspective.

All of this may make perfect sense to you.

Yet, you may be very reluctant to stop rushing around for one reason.

If you stop, you might actually *feel things*.

I know. I see you. Not only that, but I know that you might be absolutely terrified to be alone and still with your thoughts, your emotions, or even the sensations in your body.

In some cases, especially in people who develop anxiety disorders, the anxiety/fear/stress response itself becomes the new danger. Natural physical symptoms of fear and stress start to look like signs of impending disaster. Negative thoughts become twisted, magnified, and interpreted as omens, potentially nightmarish uncontrollable impulses (they are not), and signs of deteriorating sanity (they are also not). Emotions—especially "big" emotions like anger or deep sadness, instantly morph into fear. Odds are, if you are reading this book, then you are living at least some of what I am talking about. But if you are not aware of this, then let me tell you, it is not a party. It's a very difficult way to live.

Even if you are not wrestling with an anxiety disorder, you may be an over-thinker or ruminator. The stress in your life may be fueled, at least in part, by trying to solve unsolvable problems or striving to know unknowable things simply by thinking harder about them. If this is you, the idea of being left alone with those racing thoughts and the uncertainty, shame, guilt, or regret that may come with them is probably a hard "no" for you.

Don't worry.

You are not alone.

In my experience as a mental health educator, helper, and advocate for the last 10-plus years of my life, I have observed this to be the default strategy in most humans. That's because we dislike feeling the hard stuff. Everyone loves feeling happy, motivated, inspired, and validated. Nobody wants to acknowledge all the other emotions that humans are subject to feel during a lifetime.

Sadness. Disappointment. Anger. Guilt, Regret, and Shame. Loss. Grief.

> *There are many feelings most people*
> *will go to great lengths to avoid.*

We drown out our thoughts, emotions, and memories with endless social media scrolling. We live with our earbuds always inserted, frantically consuming podcasts, music, and any shred of pop culture we can dig up during every waking moment.

We drink.

We smoke.

We overeat.

We engage compulsively in "vices" like drugs, gambling, or sex.

We become obsessed with fitness, diet, or building the perfectly decorated home.

If there is a way to drown out the stuff we hate to feel or think about, humans will find it and use it. Then we'll invent new ways to steer clear of these scary thoughts and feelings and use them. This is what we do.

Frankly, our collective emotional and mental competency and resilience are rubbish. That's right, I said it. (And I even used some of my favorite British slang to do it.)

Emotional issues aside, when we slow down, we are going to feel the fear and stress even more than we usually do. Speed is an escape response, as we've seen, but in some ways, it's also a bit of a soothing response. Speed is a distraction. When you're rushing, you're hoping to grind down the fear and stress as if you're furiously rubbing it with sandpaper to make it smooth and easier to touch. We hate the gritty, rough, abrasive feeling of anxiety, fear, and stress. It is uncomfortable. We want to smooth it over and make it pleasant and easier to hold in our hands. When we slow down in the face of these things, we're allowing that rough surface to scrape against us, and we dislike that! You may be averse to the idea of slowing down simply because it feels bad.

I'm trying to get away from all these nasty feelings, and you want me to slow down, so they can catch me! WTF, Drew?

Don't worry. I've heard that about a million times.

What happens when you know you should learn to slow down, but you are afraid to because you are afraid to face … yourself?

You make a choice.

In this life, we are often faced with situations where we simply cannot have it both ways. We do not get to improve our lives and stay comfortable and cozy. Occasionally, we do, and those are good times, but in most cases, growth, change, and improvement involve some level of effort and discomfort.

Every so often, they even involve facing fear and feeling super unsteady and vulnerable.

These are the cards we've been given by the Universe. At some point, we must make a choice: stay stuck or do hard stuff and feel afraid or unsure to get un-stuck.

This is not going to turn into yet another cliché-laden life coaching manual. This is not about designing your best life (insert eye roll emoji here), but what I am about to say does need to be addressed, so stick with me for another few hundred words, then we'll get back to the good stuff, OK?

The amazing Alegra Kastens (@obsessivelyeverafter on Instagram) has been heard to say, "Suffer in the right direction."

Genius. And totally applicable in this situation.

If you spend your days rushing around in speed-demon mode, pouring fuel onto your anxiety and stress fire, you will suffer. We can argue over how much suffering you will endure, but I think we can agree that doing this is not desired or comfortable. Now, if you work on slowing down, you will wind up confronted with all the stuff you prefer not to confront. You will suffer.

Here's the choice.

Suffer one way.

Suffer the other way.

Pick one.

One changes nothing and keeps you trapped on the hamster wheel. The other gives you a chance to improve the situation to a degree. It allows for more productive, useful suffering. So, if you must suffer in some way, at least suffer in the right direction.

I won't prolong this discussion.

If you need to stop reading for a bit to get your brain around the fact that no matter what you do, you will have hard stuff to deal with, that's fine. I can wait. The book will still be here for you when you're done trying to find a way to do this without having to deal with some kind of adversity.

Spoiler alert: that way doesn't exist.

Now that we know you have a choice to make, let's move on to what it looks like when you make the choice to go Seven Percent Slower … and suffer in the right direction.

Chapter 6 — Why Go Seven Percent Slower?

We've established that your lizard brain—the fear center in your brain—has a vested interest in ordering you to speed up when responding to a perceived threat.

We know that this process is, for the most part, automatic, but that after the initial order to speed up is received, you can decide to override it and begin to slow down.

It is not easy, but it is possible.

Disobeying your lizard brain takes hard work and practice. It involves ignoring safety signals designed by thousands of years of evolution to be loud, urgent, and difficult to ignore. Disobeying your lizard brain will often make you feel unsafe, wrong, or even more stressed at first.

We will talk about that shortly.

But while the process of slowing down when your fear center is telling you otherwise is certainly difficult and often uncomfortable, it does not mean we should abandon the project.

Since you are reading *Seven Percent Slower*, I'm guessing you've already figured out that I am going to sing the praises of slowing down at some point.

This is that point.

Clearly, I am writing to get you to slow down.

But why?

You might be tempted to say that I want you to slow down to reduce your anxiety, stress, and fear levels. Close, but not exactly.

I would like you to learn how to recognize your speed reaction and slow down. This is part of an overall strategy to teach your lizard brain that it has gotten into a bad habit when it comes to misidentifying threats and sounding alarms. Slowing down shows your poor misguided lizard brain that it can take a break now and then.

I get that your objective is to reduce your anxiety, fear, and stress levels. But in my work with anxiety (see the list of resources at the end of this book for more information), I have always taught that you must first achieve an intermediate goal. That intermediate goal is the building of a new relationship with the sensations and thoughts that accompany stress, anxiety, and fear.

People—and you may be one of them—spend a huge amount of time, money, and effort to rid themselves of stress, anxiety, and fear. Many wind up making little progress or find that their ability to "make it stop" comes ... then goes. Frustration, discouragement, and a fair bit of head-scratching are involved most times. You may have tried dietary changes, meditation, crystals, talk therapy, herbs, supplements, exercise, grounding, journaling, Reiki, primal screaming, and stress reduction devices and programs, to name a few. However, here you are, likely because none of it worked consistently or with any kind of durability over time and across multiple contexts.

Here's a bit of insight for you.

Your efforts to find relief have been admirable and understandable but aimed at the wrong target.

You've been trying to eliminate the sensations and thoughts that accompany stress, anxiety, and fear. That's one reason why this approach is not working for you.

You've been trying to turn off a natural and expected part of being a human being. This isn't a good plan.

Let's assume for a second that, for some reason, you have become REALLY annoyed at the way the wheels of your car spin. You hate that spinning. It bothers you. It frightens you. Not only that, but it stresses you out when those damn wheels spin! You, therefore, do everything you can do to stop them from spinning, or at least slow them down, except you still expect the car to take you places as quickly as possible. You want to eliminate an essential part of what makes a car a car while also expecting that it will continue to work properly for you. How do you think that is going to work out for you?

This is what you're doing when you try to turn off an essential part of being human because you don't like how it feels. I'll let you chew on that for a minute or two before continuing.

At this point, you might think that I'm going to talk about finding and eliminating the "root causes" of your stress and fear, but I am not.

It is not my intention to imply that root causes are entirely meaningless. In cases where there has been real trauma or abuse in your life, the origin of your pain absolutely matters and should be addressed with professional help. I am never discounting those issues. But outside of those situations, a hard-target root cause search and destroy mission is, in most cases, another misguided effort to rid yourself of the discomfort that comes with anxiety, stress, and fear.

Do you *really* care about what's stressing you out or triggering your anxiety?

Do you *really* want to eliminate your career or any of your relationships?

Do you *really* want to remove money or social interactions from your life?

Do you *really* want to attempt to create a trigger-free existence?

I doubt that's what you want to do. I think you know that this is impractical or not desirable. Furthermore, I think you want to find your triggers because you hope that knowing them will allow you to turn off all the uncomfortable stuff that you've come to hate so much.

You try to turn off the natural response to stress, anxiety, and fear as a primary strategy. Or you try to find what triggers it, knowing that you can't eliminate every trigger but still hoping to accomplish your goal of turning off your stress/fear response in some way.

This is simply not realistic or possible. Humans feel stress, anxiety, and fear, and our bodies and minds are designed to respond to them.

So....

Now what?

If we are not here to learn how to turn off your anxiety, fear, and stress response, then what is this Seven Percent Slower thing all about? Isn't it supposed to *make you* feel better? Well, of course, it is, but before we can go there, we must work on that intermediate goal I mentioned a few paragraphs back.

1. First, you learn a new way to react and relate to your overactive fear and stress response.

2. Next, you change the way you interact with the sensations and thoughts that accompany stress, fear, and anxiety.

3. Then some magic lizard brain experiential learning happens.

4. ONLY THEN do you begin to feel better. That's how this process works—like it or not.

Your first goal is to stop being blindly dragged and ordered around by your confused lizard brain. Do that, and you can look toward that coveted "feeling better" part.

I don't doubt that you are screaming:

"OK, great! I have to learn how to respond and relate differently to the reaction that my lizard brain is demanding in such a misguided way all the time. HOW DO I DO THAT? AND WHY DO I HAVE TO DO THAT FIRST BEFORE I FEEL BETTER?"

I knew you were going to ask that.

One way you do that is to learn *how* to go Seven Percent Slower. You will want to go Seven Percent Slower because it is part of building this new reaction to and relationship with your harried lizard brain and its ancient threat defense responses. Learning to slow down helps you learn that you do not have to be dragged around anymore. It teaches you the vocabulary you need to teach your poor lizard brain so it will know that it's time to take a rest and re-evaluate its priorities.

Remember when I said that your lizard brain doesn't understand words, logic, and reason? I mentioned earlier that it is virtually impossible to TALK to your fear center, either with words or thoughts. I also touched on why this is likely an evolutionary imperative. Being able to turn off your fear response with a few words or thoughts would be a bad idea in terms of species-level survival planning. That being the case, we are left looking for some other way to communicate with your lizard brain. When it insists that you are in danger and then demands that you accelerate to ludicrous speed, how will you tell it otherwise? (Bonus points if you get the "ludicrous speed" reference.)

Enter Seven Percent Slower.

When you slow down, you act in opposition to what your hyperactive lizard brain wants you to do. It wants you to speed up to remain safe. Comply and wind up in speed-demon mode, trying to talk yourself, and your activated lizard brain off the ledge, and your circumstances will not change in any meaningful way. You answer the demand for speed by accelerating, then attempt to use all manner of soothing and calming techniques to quiet your five-alarm brain. This does not work, or it may only work temporarily. You know the drill: calm yourself at 2 PM, wind up feeling like you've been shot out of a cannon again by 5 PM.

When you disobey your lizard brain's demand for speed, when you choose to slow down instead, you are responding to that demand with language that your fear center can understand.
You are speaking its language—the language of behavior and action and experience.

When you go Seven Percent Slower, you can actually communicate with your lizard brain. You gain the ability to talk to it through behavioral signaling and experiences. Where all those words and mantras and herbs and crystals and soothing rituals failed, simply behaving differently—going Seven Percent Slower—gets the job done.

Do not misunderstand me. This is not an instant cure for the anxiety, stress, or fear dominating your life. Slowing things down will not instantly and permanently pacify your overactive fear center. There is no magic in slowing down. It is not a shield against anxiety or stress. Seven Percent Slower is a tool. It is part of a new and more productive way to relate to this part of your humanity. It is effective but going Seven Percent Slower will not instantly flip off the anxiety or stress switch. Going Seven Percent Slower is a way to TEACH your lizard brain how it can correct the course it is on and how it can change the way it operates. But this takes time.

You can teach an old lizard brain new tricks,
but not overnight. It can be a slow learner,
but it can learn. Trust me on this. Be patient.

Going Seven Percent Slower is NOT easy at first. When your brain screams at you to run away, and instead you relax your body, lengthen your stride, and slow everything down, you ignore and disobey survival instincts. This is a difficult concept to make peace with and an even more difficult concept to master. Luckily, difficult does not mean impossible. It merely means challenging. I'm confident you are up for this challenge.

When you accept this idea and begin to implement it, going Seven Percent Slower plays a key role in teaching your hyperactive threat response center that it can stand down and take a break. You can't TELL it to knock off early and go home to watch Netflix. You can only SHOW it that it is safe to do so, then continue to show it repeatedly to drive home the point.

When you break it down, the Seven Percent Slower concept is simple.

1. Your lizard brain needs behavioral signals and experiences to process.

2. Acceleration signals danger.

3. Slowing down signals that everything is OK. Your job is to start feeding your lizard brain a steady stream of "all clear" signals.

This is why I urge you to learn how to go Seven Percent Slower. Making this change in your life is an act of compassion toward your overworked fear center. Make the effort to teach it this new language, so it doesn't have to be so wound up and on guard all the time.

Learn to go Seven Percent Slower.

Let your tired, stressed, overworked brain kick back a bit, and your life will begin to get better.

I promise it will still be there for you when the chips are down—when and if you need protection.

But it doesn't have to run itself—and you—ragged for no good reason for the rest of your life.

Chapter 7 — Is This Mindfulness? Do I Have to Meditate?

Kind of … and not necessarily. Sorry to be as clear as mud. Let me explain.

We hear about mindfulness all the damn time. If you have any bit of interest in the mental health, personal development, or self-help space online, you are seeing the word *mindfulness* no less than a dozen times every day. Mindfulness is often held up as a panacea. It is the cure for everything. Learning to live in this ideal moment-to-moment existence will set you free, right? Be mindful! Then all your stress, anxiety, and fear will magically melt away; you'll float through life without a care in the world (insert exploding head emoji here).

In theory, that is not entirely wrong. Too often, the concept of mindfulness becomes a source of confusion and overwhelm for the average person just trying to find a better way to manage a stressful or anxious life. When buried under a mountain of Instagram posts featuring placid ponds and Thich Nhat

Hanh quotes, it's easy to conclude that living mindfully requires a dramatic spiritual and structural shift. In reality, this can seem impossible to achieve.

Telling an overachieving business owner or a person gripped by panic disorder that they need to be "in the moment" seems like a good idea, but it can often fill those people with a combination of disbelief, dread, and frustration. Trust me. I was both of them.

If you are struggling with an overly stressful or anxious life, you do not have to suddenly learn to "go deep within" to change things. You are not required to chant, ground, vibrate, or commune with spirit animals to improve your situation. No major shift in worldview, spirituality, or energy flow is required. You can make use of tools like mindfulness and meditation using simple and easy-to-implement methods, and they will help.

In a nutshell, you do not have to become perfectly mindful. You just have to become MORE mindful than you have been. That's all. You don't need perfection—just improvement. Learning how to go Seven Percent Slower can help get you there.

What is mindfulness?

What is meditation?

Thousands of books have been written on these topics, so I will not re-invent that wheel. But I do want to spend some time clarifying what these two terms mean in this particular context. I am only concerned with your first moves toward more mindful living and in teaching you how to make those easy-to-understand and implement moves. You may find that you enjoy learning to be more mindful in the way you live your life. You may find that you like meditation as a continued practice. That's excellent. There are many great resources to learn from, follow, and grow with. But for now, we will stick to the basics of what we need for our purposes.

Mindfulness is simply the state of being fully engaged with what is happening NOW, rather than reviewing the past or predicting the future. We do not qualify our mindfulness.

It is not mandatory to appreciate the here and now, to find any special meaning or beauty in it, or to be grateful for any of it.

That is simply not required for our purposes. Thinking we need to do more than what's needed may put people off and can seem intimidating for a total beginner. Telling a stressed or fearful person that gratitude is the answer is getting a bit old. You may feel grateful, or you may not. This may change from minute to minute. That's perfectly fine. There is no special quality of mindfulness that we are seeking.

I also need to point out that you do not need to figure out what "being present" means. You only need to be engaged. "Present" is esoteric and wrapped in amorphous spirituality and new-agey stuff. "Engaged" is practical. You do not need to be present. You only have to pay attention to what is going on now. Attention is the operative concept in our mindfulness. Attention is where it's at. You know what paying attention means. You don't have to learn anything new to do that. You only have to practice and get good at it.

Speaking of attention, let's define meditation. Meditation is not spiritual, energetic, or some special way to connect you to the Universe. Meditation is only a way to learn to train your focus and … wait for it … your ATTENTION. We will think of meditation as the practice of learning to train your attention on a selected point.

If you are reading this book, odds are your attention is all over the place. You are trying to pay attention to life, but life consists of a million constant swirling targets. Your attention might be bouncing like a ping pong ball from one life issue to another all day long. This is common, and it contributes to the frenzied mental state that your hyper-aware lizard brain has decided is worthy of the danger response. When you "can't turn your brain off," everything feels overwhelming. When you feel overwhelmed, things feel beyond your control. Being tossed about without having any control gets interpreted as a threat, and you know now what that means in terms of how you feel.

Now let's add the stress, anxiety, and fear responses themselves. Those are SERIOUSLY unpleasant.

The twist in your stomach.

The burning in your gut.

The pounding of your heart.

The shaking of your hands.

The feeling of being unbalanced or dizzy.

The sensation of a metal band tightening around your chest.

These are natural, but they are not pleasant. However, they are attention and focus magnets! When you're having a difficult enough time paying attention to your life effectively, the extra stress and anxiety response guzzle your attention the way a 17-year-old boy with a fake ID guzzles cheap beers.

At the moment, paying attention and getting focused is likely a problem for you. In this context, meditation is just a way to work on that.

Nothing more.

Meditation is like the gym for your attention and focus muscles. For our purposes, learning basic meditation and practicing it daily just means learning to let the extraneous stuff come and go (NOT stopping it) while you bring your attention to where you want it to be. Sounds pretty basic, right?

It is!

Of course, this does not make it easy to learn or master. Like any new skill, it must be practiced, and you will likely be awful at it when you start. But in the end, meditation isn't a big hazy mystery. It's a simple tool that we will use to help you go Seven Percent Slower when you need and want to.

There. That's mindfulness and meditation in our world. Doesn't sound so complicated, does it?

How Does Going Seven Percent Slower Relate to Mindfulness and Meditation?

You will find that the relation between Seven Percent Slower, mindfulness, and meditation is in the resulting reduction of your rushing and overall speed.

When you learn to recognize your rushing habits and slow things down methodically and repeatedly, you almost have no choice from an operational standpoint but to come face-to-face with what is happening in the present moment. Slowing down will automatically connect you more closely to the here-and-now by shifting your attention to what you are engaged with at the moment and away from a prediction of the future or a rumination over the past.

Slowing down means putting the brakes on your accidental emergency multitasking.

What Is "Accidental Emergency Multitasking"?

Accidental emergency multitasking means you enter into a very high anxiety or stress state and try to do EVERYTHING all at the same time. You bounce from thought to thought (and fear to fear) in rapid sequence. You swing back and forth from thinking and inward focus to trying to rapidly DO things with an outward focus and back again. You try to say every word you want to say immediately upon thinking them while at the same time fixating on the past and future, fumbling with your keys, the pen in your hand, the paper you're trying to write, the book you're trying to read, and the conversation you're trying to listen to.

It is not your intention to get into this frantic state where you are trying to force everything to happen rapidly and immediately, yet you enter into it when anxious and afraid.

You sense an emergency. You begin to multitask (poorly, if you are like most people in this state) without really thinking about it.

Emergency.

Accidental.

Multitasking.

This is an overly complicated and complex state to be in. Think about it. When you get into that mode, the feeling of being overwhelmed shifts to front and center. Everything bleeds together into a frenzied cacophony of thoughts, sights, sounds, and sensations where you're tracking past, present, and future all at the same time. Or at least trying.

Intentionally slowing down simplifies the situation. Purposely doing only one task at a time and paying attention to it means that you stop ruminating and predicting while also trying to handle the current moment. This causes you to wind up in the current moment both intentionally and accidentally. That moment may involve speaking, listening, or doing something behaviorally. It may involve thinking. Yes, thinking is allowed. We are learning to focus our attention on one thing at a time—thoughts included.

When you slow down by Seven Percent,
you have no choice but to become aware of the
current moment and engage in whatever is
happening in that moment.

Do you know what that means?

It means you'll manage to be mindful without trying to be mindful. Let me clarify that. You won't automatically achieve guru-level mindfulness. You'll just be MORE mindful than you are usually, and that's all you need.

Think of Seven Percent Slower as the more practical, easy-to-open back door to mindfulness and meditation. No pillows, incense, chanting, or bogus Morgan Freeman internet memes required. Just some common-sense, practical tools to learn and practice.

Mindfulness and meditation benefits without
all that pesky mindfulness and meditation!
Sounds halfway decent, doesn't it?
Trust me. It really is.

NOTE: I am a massive fan of regular meditation practice, but you do not have to sit cross-legged on pillows for an hour every day to learn to slow down. We'll talk about the use of meditation later on but suffice to say that it will not be a requirement or a lynchpin of this concept.

Chapter 8 — Learning To Go Seven Percent Slower: Acknowledging

First, let's acknowledge that going Seven Percent Slower isn't practically possible.

WHAT? All these words to tell me that this is impossible? I want a refund!

Hang on a minute.

Before you storm the castle, hear me out.

The term "Seven Percent Slower" is a useful mental trick to keep you mindful of your rushing and acceleration habits. Remembering to go "Seven Percent" Slower is a good way to remember that you must slow down to some degree.

Why seven percent?

No real reason.

It seems an odd enough number to be intellectually and mentally interesting while also being a bit absurd. If you know me, you know that I am a fan of the absurd. Silly things are easy to remember. They resonate with us. They stay with us. So, I picked the number seven out of thin air because it seemed just right.

In practice, you cannot go Seven Percent Slower. It's simply not practical or even possible in most cases. I don't want you getting all worked up over having to do some new math on the fly to calculate how quickly you're moving through the school pick-up line. That isn't required. You may wind up going three percent slower or 17 percent slower. Both are fine.

You don't have to be perfectly slow. Just slower than usual. See how this theme keeps repeating?

All we care about here is that you use the concept of going Seven Percent Slower as a reminder to slow down when you're itching to kick into speed-demon mode. How much you slow down will vary from day to day or even hour to hour, but if you're going slower than you used to, you're winning!

Now that we have that out of the way, let's talk about what acknowledging stuff means. Acknowledging certain things—noticing them—is the first part of learning to go Seven Percent Slower.

Acknowledge that up to this point, you have been unaware of the choices and control you have when anxious, afraid, or stressed, or that you have chosen to disregard these things. Either way, you have seen yourself as powerless in the face of anxiety, fear, and stress. You've been working under the assumption that you have no control and MUST obey your anxious and fear-driven thoughts. After you acknowledge this, then you can move on to acknowledging that you are *wrong.*

You may think that everything "goes out the window" when you feel stress or fear, but this is not true. You are simply having a more difficult time making choices and acting rationally. This does not mean that you are totally incapacitated in those moments. You may not make the fastest choices or act totally rationally, but choice, control, and reason are still available to you, even when you feel like you are at your wit's end. Whoever told you that you must be the best possible version of yourself to be capable was wrong. Even when your ability to reason, act, and make choices is impaired, the ability still exists.

Stumbling over words is still speaking.

Trembling legs can still walk.

An anxious mind can still function.

Maybe not perfectly, but again, we don't need perfection. We rarely do.

Acknowledge that you are wrong when you declare that anxiety, fear, and stress can nail to you a post and control you completely. This is your first major acknowledgment along the way to going Seven Percent Slower.

Next, work on acknowledging the situation you are in. Rather than allowing moments of anxiety, fear, and stress to be vaguely defined disasters, see them for what they are. Acknowledge the facts of the situation. Do not simply declare, "Oh no, here we go again!", try this instead:

"I am anxious, afraid, or stressed now. This can happen to humans. Sometimes for obvious reasons. Sometimes for reasons we do not immediately know. But it happens, it's natural, and right now, it's happening to me."

Can you see how taking a second to acknowledge the situation objectively rather than emotionally can help point you in the right direction?

Next, you need to acknowledge the role of your lizard brain —your fear center. Remember that your lizard brain is there to do a job. It wants to keep you safe, and it will use all the resources at its disposal to get that job done. Rather than throwing your hands up because you hate how your body responds to a perceived threat, take a moment to acknowledge what's really happening. While you do that, turn your attention to the speed and rushing issue.

Try saying, "My lizard brain is sending instructions to my body to react to this situation. It wants to keep me safe, which is natural. It wants me to speed up now because that is part of the mechanism of seeking safety. This is normal and natural, and I can't stop it. I can only work with it constructively to change things over time. Remember when I made a list of my rushing habits? I now have a choice. Do I want to make one of those choices, or not?"

The final acknowledgment you must make is the need to send the right signals back down the chain to your fear center. Remember that speed breeds more speed. Rushing around tells your lizard brain that you are still in danger and should continue to rush around until safe. But since there is no danger to escape, the rushing gets you nowhere. Your job is to signal that there is no danger, that the alarm was not needed.

How do you do this?

By going slower than your lizard brain wants you to go. Seven Percent Slower. Your final acknowledgment looks something like this:

"I need to send a signal to my lizard brain that the current problem or situation I am facing is not an actual threat and does not warrant this ancient fight or flight response! I can do this by slowing down. Speed signals danger. Going slower signals safety. I need to SHOW my poor lizard brain that it can take a break now."

Now I need to make another point. If you've heard me speak or have read anything I've ever written about anxiety, you'll know I constantly say that we cannot talk ourselves out of feeling anxiety, panic, fear, or stress. This is still true. Yet here I am, giving you all the self-talk acknowledgment to do so! The thing is, I am not advocating self-talk in any way. Will you be talking to yourself in some way? Of course, you will. But do you see any mention of self-soothing, trying to convince yourself that you are OK, or trying to talk away the stress, fear, or anxiety?

You do not.

So, while I do acknowledge that this may seem a bit confusing, in reality, this set of basic acknowledgments is not designed as self-talk or soothing. Rather, it is designed to prime ACTION.

These statements are designed to pre-empt your usual "OMG!" response, but that's not where it ends. We want to inhibit that old response—which includes the speeding up and rushing around—so we can put a new plan into action. While it may look like you are engaging in five minutes of inner dialogue and deliberation, you'll be learning that the mental acknowledgments happen rapidly.

When you practice this new habit enough, you will notice your anxious, stressed-out state, and you *will* move through your required acknowledgments within seconds. Then you will use that to inform a new set of actions. Slower actions. Seven Percent Slower actions. The whole sequence will happen in less time than it took you to read this paragraph. I promise. Even your anxious, stressed-out brain is MUCH faster than you think it is.

Acknowledgment Homework

The world of Cognitive Behavior Therapy has excellent cognitive restructuring and reframing exercises that a good therapist will give you to do. These might be done in-session at first, but most times, they will be homework for you. Cognitive restructuring and reframing is effective. Not by itself. Action is needed. New behavioral patterns are the key to success but working on reframing things is a helpful adjunct.

To be clear, you cannot simply restructure your thoughts on demand, especially when you are in the middle of an anxiety spike rooted in the overwhelm of stress or fear. It won't work. This is not about learning to "change your mindset" to banish anxiety or stress on the spot. I will never get behind that plan.

What I am offering here is an easy way to practice going through the precursor acknowledgments that we need to slow things down when the situation warrants it. If you practice this approach when calm and peaceful, it becomes far easier to remember what to do when you're in a heightened state.

There are a few ways you can work through these precursor acknowledgments.

You may choose to write them down. This is like studying. Anyone who has ever studied for exams knows that one of the most useful study tools is copying notes that you've already taken. Many a student has spent many a dollar on stacks of index cards and used them to write important concepts, so they can leaf through them regularly. Yes, I said index cards. I'm dating myself, but so be it.

Try writing your Seven Percent Slower acknowledgments on a set of index cards. You'll only need a few cards. You could also use a notebook. Then flip through them a few times each day. It only takes a minute or two, and it is an effective way to drill these concepts into your brain. You could type them into a series of notes on your phone or tablet if you choose to. But I am told by some brilliant people that the act of writing something manually is a more effective learning tool, so I am suggesting that you write them down, then read them back to yourself regularly.

You may choose to scrawl them somewhere so that you see them throughout your day. A note on the fridge is common. Some people will stick a reminder on the bathroom mirror or even write in lipstick on the mirror. I know people who attach sticky notes to the dashboard in the car to remind them of important items. All of these are good ways to learn and remember your precursor acknowledgments.

Finally, say the acknowledgments out loud a few times every day. You might say them into a mirror, while you are driving by yourself, while cooking dinner, or taking your daily walk. While I don't love this method and haven't found it useful, many people have, so it is worth giving it a try. It certainly can't hurt.

Remember that these are not mantras or affirmations. *These are operational concepts that you will use to enact a behavioral change in your response to anxiety, fear, and stress.* You are not learning the acknowledgments for any other reason than to prime yourself for action when you need to slow down rather than rushing around like you are trying to escape a burning building. I cannot stress this enough. **Expectation and intent really matter, so stay on track**.

OK, What's Next?

In Chapter 9, we'll talk about the actual behavioral changes you can make to learn to go Seven Percent Slower in the face of anxiety, stress, and fear. For now, we've placed you on some new footing, ready to make those changes.

1. You are not powerless in the face of anxiety, fear, and stress. You are still capable, even if your behaviors are not perfect.

2. You can acknowledge being anxious, afraid, and stressed out without declaring it to be a disaster. You can assess tense situations more objectively and less emotionally.

3. When keyed up, you know that your body is reacting to a perceived threat in a normal, natural, predictable way. This includes the demand to speed things up! You are no longer going to try to squash that response or instantly banish it. Instead, you are going to make a conscious choice to slow down to help calm your overactive lizard brain over time.

4. You will now work at sending behavioral signals back down the line to your lizard brain. Going Seven Percent Slower is one of those signals. You now know that this is your job and why you are going to work on making that choice.

This is a good place to be, so let's move on!

Chapter 9 — Learning To Go Seven Percent Slower: Action

Time to take action!

This chapter is where you will change your behavior to slow things down by seven percent. Remember that you can't go exactly Seven Percent Slower. It would be almost impossible to measure that and totally impractical to implement. I just use the term "Seven Percent Slower" as an easy-to-remember concept that acts as a general reminder to SLOW DOWN.

When I talk about going Seven Percent Slower, I often get two types of feedback:

1. "This is spectacular! It's making a huge difference in my ability to handle anxiety and stress!"

2. "This makes sense, but HOW do I go slower? I just can't help myself. I wind up rushing around like a chicken with no head!"

If you are person number one, then thank you for buying and reading this book, even though you might not need it. You already grasp the concept of going Seven Percent Slower, and you're working on using it as a tool in your plan to better navigate through the anxiety and stress in your life. Excellent!

If you are person number two, this chapter is for you. You want to go Seven Percent Slower because you want to ultimately feel better. But as much as you want this, you feel like you just don't know how to do it. If you've read this far, and you're happy because we're getting to the point where we learn how to go Seven Percent Slower, first let me remind you of two things:

Chapter 5 of this book is all about why you might not want to go slower. If you're still in that mode where you're afraid to actually feel the sensations of anxiety, fear, and stress, then I understand why this is a hard sell for you. Go back and re-read that chapter a few times if you need to.

Chapter 8 of this book specifically addresses the "but I can't" notion. Trust me. You CAN. You are not completely incapacitated by how you feel. You might feel impaired, but you're not incapacitated. Circle back and re-read Chapter 8 if you need to before going on.

The Mechanics of Going Seven Percent Slower

Fortunately, this is not that complicated. You may find yourself wondering where all the "stuff" is, but the truth is that there really isn't a ton of stuff to present here. This is simple, but simple is good. We like simple!

Simple, however, does not mean easy. Remember, as you practice this new approach that you will likely fall back into your old rushing habit again and again. Learning to go against your lizard brain—slowing down when it tells you to speed up—is not an easy task. This is like learning a brand-new language. You will make mistakes. You will stumble. You will get it "wrong" lots of times. Just keep practicing and working at it. This is a new skill for you. We must learn and practice new skills before we are good at them. It's part of being human. Allow yourself to be human!

If you've read my other books or heard me speak, you are going to recognize the first few concepts here. Yes, I talk about them all the time. There is a reason for that.

Release the Tension in Your Body

It is very difficult to slow down when you are wound up and ready to pop. When you realize that you are in Speed-Racer mode, your first job is to release the tension in your body. Doing this takes repetition. Calm and relaxed are two different things, so it will feel like a struggle, but you must learn that you CAN relax your body even when you are not calm. I promise you can do it. Real people do it, I swear. It will feel impossible at first and even scary. But when you realize that you are rushing around, do your best to go as limp as your situation allows (clearly, you cannot let go of the steering wheel while driving).

Are your shoulders up around your ears?

Are you bracing your abdominal muscles like you're expecting a punch to the gut?

Are you clenching your jaw or digging your fingers into your palms?

Are you squinting or grimacing?

How is your ... um .... rear end (such an awkward question!)? Are you tensing those muscles?

These are common tension points for most people. Be aware of them and release that tension. Do it over and over. When you feel these tension points clenching up, release them. Sometimes you won't even feel that you are flexing those muscles because doing this has become an automatic response for you.

That is OK.

When you notice that you are rushing again, also notice if you're tensed up. If you are, release. Rushing and physical tension often come in the same package, so your level of "rushing-ness" will be a good indicator of how tense your body is. Use this to your advantage, so you can release that tension as best you can and as many times as you need to.

Maybe you are like many people who get frustrated and say:

"I try to go limp, but I can't."

Often this means that you are not even sure of what physical relaxation is supposed to feel like. You may have a habit of tensing up all day long, so releasing that tension may feel strange and unfamiliar to you, which can lead you to conclude that you are "doing it wrong." Let me assure you; this is very common. Do not let frustration overwhelm you. Later on, I will give you some things you can practice to improve at this exercise over time. Patience, grasshopper. You are learning new things!

Breathe

Man, I hate even writing that line.

"Breathe" is such an overused, clichéd bit of advice. Half the time, when someone tells you to "just breathe," they are speaking to you on auto-pilot because it's what we say to sound like Zen masters. I am not telling you to breathe because there is some kind of magic in your breath.

I suppose it's possible that your breath is laced with jasmine and peppermint and smells like the dreams of an angel, but even if this is the case, it is still not magic in any way.

For our purposes, breathing is simply a tool. It seems slightly crazy to have to "use" breath, given that it is an essential and automatic bodily function at the most basic level, but we do. And we need to talk about your breath because you are likely doing one of two things when you get anxious, afraid, or stressed out. Both of them are not helping you slow down. In fact, they are fueling the rushing and acceleration response and ramping up the sensations that come with anxiety, fear, and stress.

You are likely either holding your breath or over-breathing, aka hyperventilating.

Breath-holding was my jam. I was a world-class breath holder, baby! I would rush around, stumbling and bumping into things, trying desperately to escape from all those awful anxiety and fear sensations and thoughts. And ... I was holding my breath.

You may be, too.

If you find that you are suddenly aware that you "can't breathe," this is very likely the result of you NOT breathing for the last 20-30 seconds. At some point, your body is going to force you to breathe, and when it does, it isn't pretty. Holding your breath causes a build-up of carbon dioxide in your bloodstream. Your heart rate increases. You get tighter. Anyone who has tried to win a breath-holding contest with a friend knows what I'm talking about. When you finally must give in and breathe again, you gasp a bit, and your body is the *opposite* of relaxed. This is not dangerous because your body knows how to correct this quickly, but when you hold your breath, you are creating an environment in your body that screams "DANGER!" and you know who is listening to that. That's right. Mr. Lizard Brain hears that signal loud and clear. He's an eavesdropper.

Over-breathing usually looks like trying to get that "deep cleansing/grounding breath" ... over and over. How many times in your life have you been told to "take a deep breath" when you're stressed out and people are trying to calm you down?

For some reason, we have decided that totally filling our lungs to capacity, then exhaling like we're trying to blow down a brick wall, is a calming tool.

Taking a deep breath and exhaling with force won't do any harm. But when you are in an anxious, fearful, or stressed state, and you repeatedly try to calm or soothe yourself with these magical breaths, things get wonky quickly.

Most people think that over-breathing means panting like a dog. It does, but it also means repeated large breaths with rapid high-volume exhalations. The stress-driven "cleansing breath" is a great example. That giant exhale that follows the giant inhale blows off a ton of carbon dioxide in one shot. Do that a few times in a short period, and you will get a bit light-headed and feel strange. Feeling light-headed, dizzy, and un-real is not a recipe for going slower in any way. Why? Because those are danger signals for your fear center to intercept and act upon. Over-breathing is a bad habit because it sends you in the opposite direction that you want to be going in.

So … breathe. When you find yourself holding your breath, stop. When you find yourself engaging in a series of extra deep breaths and heavy sighs hoping to calm down, stop. Just breathe in a natural rhythm. This is very difficult because when you focus on breathing "naturally," it will initially feel anything but natural. It will feel forced and awkward and sometimes like you've for-gotten how to breathe. This is very common. Do not worry. There is a simple way to get back to your regular pace of breathing.

Inhale.

Through your nose if possible.

You do NOT have to fill your lungs to capacity on every breath.

When you inhale, expand your belly.

Do not move your shoulders or chest.

Hold for literally a second or so. No more.

Exhale. Through your mouth if possible.

Your exhalation should be slow and controlled and should last longer than your inhalation by a second or two.

Repeat.

That's it. That's how you will breathe when working on going Seven Percent Slower. Breathe into your belly and let your exhalation be slow and longer than your inhalation. Some people find that it helps to count on the inhalation and exhalation. In for five, out for seven. In for four, out for six. The actual numbers don't matter. Pick a rhythm that feels right for you, and understand that breathing is a dynamic thing. Sometimes four and six will be appropriate. Sometimes five and seven. It will vary. Just work on not holding your breath, not over-breathing, and breathing like I just taught you.

Similar to releasing the tension in your body, correcting your breathing with this method may feel awkward and difficult at first. That's OK. Learning new things takes time. Breaking old habits takes time. Don't beat yourself up if you fall into old breath habits every so often. That's bound to happen. Later on,

I will give you some pointers to practice improving your breathing. These are small tips, but they go a long way toward helping you slow things down.

Know Where You Want Your Attention To Be. Then Put It There.

When anxious, afraid, or stressed, you will have a propensity to engage in an extended inner dialogue about how you feel. You will chat with yourself about what is bothering you, all the possible solutions to all your current problems, and why those problems exist to begin with. You may feel like your brain "won't turn off." Furthermore, you may be in the habit of constantly analyzing and attempting mental problem-solving. Needing to know. Needing to figure out. Needing to fix.

We can call it rumination.

We can call it obsession.

We can call it brain race.

We can call it any number of things.

The label doesn't matter.

Part of your anxiety and stress response is probably an exaggerated INWARD focus on your thoughts, the feelings in your body, and the specifics of your situation. When your lizard brain signals a threat and starts the launch sequence in your body and mind, you probably launch into analysis and problem-solving mode. This is not terribly helpful, so we must address it as we start to go Seven Percent Slower.

Let me elaborate. If there is an elephant standing on your foot, thinking about ways to move that elephant is an excellent idea. If someone is pointing a gun at you, using your brainpower to figure out how to disarm that person or escape will come in handy. But in our context, when there is no actual immediate threat, and your lizard brain is firing in response to general life stressors or normal anxiety sensations, going inward and thinking excessively will make things worse.

Why will it make things worse? Because when you find yourself amped up physically and rushing around because you are anxious, afraid, or stressed out without an immediate and present threat, you will attempt to solve a problem that is likely unsolvable at that moment. You will attempt to banish a threat that does not exist. You will attempt to know things that are probably unknowable, at least at that moment. When your inward focus and thinking prove fruitless because they do not solve your problem, remove the perceived threat, or make you feel better, often you will attempt to think HARDER or LOUDER. That doesn't work either—because it was never going to work.

When this happens, you will find yourself in an even more amplified threat response mode—showing your lizard brain that there IS a threat and that try as you may, you cannot escape from it. What do you think Mr. Lizard Brain is going to do with that signal? Sure enough, he is going to turn up the volume on you. This is not helpful as we are trying to teach him that it is OK to turn DOWN the volume.

I am not saying that you should never think about your problems or your life. I am not saying that you must spend your days in a thoughtless, mindless, zombie state. I am simply stating that when you are dealing with anxiety and stress at a level that is impacting your well-being and how you function daily, you need to acknowledge the role of excessive inward focus and thinking as a contributing factor to that extreme state. When you find yourself rushing around, as you are working on going Seven Percent Slower to improve things, you will need to change where you put your attention in those moments.

Rather than paying attention to how your body feels, pay attention to what you are doing. Rather than paying attention to the mental replay of yesterday's marketing meeting that you fear went so badly, pay attention to where you are now. Rather than paying attention to the laundry list of major life changes you think you need to make immediately, pay attention to what you want to be doing in the present.

Pick a focus for your attention.

The shopping you are doing.

The email you are writing.

The song you are listening to.

The bike you are riding.

The conversation you are presently engaged in.

It doesn't really matter. Pick a thing you are doing right now. If you are not doing anything because you are living in your head and ruminating, then pick something you *want* to do or *need* to do. Do *anything* other than scanning your body and engaging in extended inner dialogue.

When you've established that focal point, do your best to keep your attention there. Know that you will get sucked back into your head now and then. This is normal. Humans think, especially when we are convinced that thinking is helping us or keeping us "safe." When you find yourself focusing inward, move your focus and attention gently back out to the task at hand, whatever that may be.

Exaggerate Your Physical Slowness When Moving Through Space and Time

The first three items on our Seven Percent Slower list:

1. Releasing tension,

2. Breathing, and

3. Focusing your attention—are all ways to help "prime the pump."

They help create a framework for you to work in when moving Seven Percent Slower. But by themselves, they are not necessarily ways to slow down. We have to do more to work on truly slowing things down physically and behaviorally.

This is the part where you learn to go Seven Percent Slower. Well, not actually seven percent, but slower than you've been going, and that's what counts!

At this point, you've read approximately 17,000 words leading up to the point of actually getting the "tips" on how to move more slowly through space and time. In reality, there aren't that many tips. Moving more slowly is literally just that. Moving more slowly.

The biggest "tip" I can give you is … EXAGGERATE!

Seriously.

When you think you're moving slowly, move *more* slowly. I am not dooming you to a life that looks like a super slow-motion video. However, it is important for you to recognize that when learning to break the speed habit, you will need to *really* exaggerate that slowness to find a meaningful drop in your pace.

Virtually every new skill we learn in life involves starting with exaggerated, deliberate movements and actions. When learning scales, my guitar teacher had me go VERY slowly to start. I was taught to concentrate on every movement of my fingers on the fretboard, paying attention to proper technique and positioning. Singers learn to exaggerate when moving their mouths and faces to form the words they are singing. When learning a new language, we speak it slowly and with an exaggerated accent. Learning to dribble a basketball is slow and deliberate at first. You get the idea.

In each of the cases above, the initial action is awkward and unnatural. There's nothing fluid or graceful about it, but that's the way it has to be.

Natural, fluid, and graceful come later.

If you think that slowing your body down is supposed to make you look like a Zen master in motion on day one, think again. This is not a spiritual ballet. This is a bit ugly. Frankly, it will feel weird to you. That's OK. Learning new things, breaking old habits, and building new ones are often awkward. There's no crime in feeling odd when you do this.

I'm going to take the awkwardness to an even higher level. I want you to exaggerate your slowness to such a point that it becomes comical to you. When you get to the point where it feels totally absurd and ridiculous, you know you're moving slowly. When you want to burst into laughter at yourself because what you are doing seems so silly, you've arrived.

This is the point at which you can dial back the exaggeration a bit. You don't have to stay there. But I do want you to try this quite often in the early days of going Seven Percent Slower. To achieve the desired speed (or lack thereof), you need to overshoot it, then allow for your natural tendency to rush to bring you back to where you want to be.

To put things into the context of the book title, if you want to go Seven Percent Slower, you'll have to practice going maybe 11 percent slower, then let nature take its course. The exaggeration will be an important tool when you first start making this speed shift; then, it will become a corrective tool when you find yourself slipping back into old habits. More on this in a bit when we talk about the feedback/checking mechanism.

What does learning to go Seven Percent Slower look like?

 When you reach for your coffee cup, reach for it in slow motion, or what feels like slow motion to you.

 When you are putting on your shoes, put them on in slow motion.

 When you chew your food, chew in slow motion.

 When you walk, walk in slow motion. Be aware of each step and each time your foot connects with the ground. Slow down enough to actually feel that.

 When you speak, speak more slowly.

 When you brush your teeth, brush in slow motion.

 When you are opening the door to your car to get in and drive away, perform that action in slow motion.

 When you are taking laundry out of the clothes dryer, take one item out at a time, fold it, then move to the next. Move slowly.

 When you are planting vegetables in your garden, plant each one slowly and deliberately. Plant in slow motion.

 When you are painting the wall in your bedroom, move the roller or paint brush slowly and deliberately. Paint in slow motion.

Are you getting the idea? The above are all perfect examples of regular life activities that can be done Seven Percent Slower. Each gives you an opportunity to try this new slowness on for size. See how it feels. Give it a spin around the block. Get the hang of it.

As you can see by now, going Seven Percent Slower as part of your new reaction and relationship with anxiety, fear, and stress is not something you only do when anxious, afraid, or stressed. Especially when trying to build this new habit and skill, you must try this and practice it as often as you can. Take the opportunity to practice your new slowness whenever you can. It will matter. If you don't practice eating breakfast more slowly, it will be more difficult to use that skill when you are afraid, anxious, or stressed out.

I will admit that I have racked my brain a bit while writing this book to come up with some creative ways to teach you how to move more slowly. But in the end, moving more slowly is simply that. Moving more slowly. You can do that. You know what it looks like to go slowly. You just have to actually do it, practice it and exaggerate it to get the real feel of it. I could probably write another 100,000 words attempting to teach you how to move more slowly, but in the end, words are not ideally suited to this task. The best way for you to learn to move more slowly—Seven Percent more slowly—is to try it and do it again and again.

The Feedback Loop. Checking Your Speed

When I was working almost full time to recover from my anxiety disorders and using Seven Percent Slower as a tool, one useful trick I developed was to create a bit of a checking/feedback system. When I would go into my planned exposure sessions, I would use my then fancy first-generation iPhone to set a 90-second repeating timer. I would start the timer so that every 90 seconds, I got an audible alert that would remind me to check my speed and slow down again.

This proved to be VERY useful! I was finding that despite my best intentions, I would slow down for a few seconds, then get swept up by the anxiety and become a tensed-up speed demon again in short order. Rather than relying on my overloaded brain to catch it consistently, I used the mechanism of the 90-second timer to remind me to slow down. It worked very well for me.

I used the 90-second timer for a week or two during my planned exposure sessions, and any time I found myself in the grips of high anxiety. During that time, my work was clearly focused on slowing down above all else because the damn timer honked at me every 90 seconds. At times, it frustrated me. It felt like I was spending too much time focused on slowing down and not enough on actually "getting better at anxiety."

I was wrong.

After two weeks or so of determined slow-moving, I discovered I was having an easier time slowing down, maintaining a mellower speed, and that I did not need a timer every 90 seconds anymore.

At that point, I stretched the timer to three minutes. I kept it there for another two weeks or so as a reminder. That was also helpful, but admittedly, I am a fast learner and adapt quickly, so I really didn't need the timer in those second two weeks as much as I needed it in the beginning.

I finally moved my timer to five minutes, but I rarely needed it at that point. Four to six weeks of building a new habit with constant practice using this little feedback/checking habit did the job. I was consistently maintaining a slower, more relaxed pace through my exposure sessions and when anxious and afraid in general.

Did that cure my anxiety?
No. It did not.
Seven Percent Slower is not a cure for anxiety or stress.
It is ***one*** *tool in your toolbox.*

In my experience, consistently slowing down and maintaining a more relaxed state even when not calm (relaxed and calm are not the same) helped me accelerate my recovery progress. As my lizard brain got the safety message more consistently from me, my anxiety and panic felt a bit less scary. I could move more quickly up my fear-exposure ladder. If you have no idea what I'm talking about, that either means that you are not dealing with an anxiety disorder (this is good), or you are and have not yet learned the best way to go up the ladder. If this is you, you can find out more on my website at theanxioustruth.com.

My suggestion here is that you implement my little timer mechanism the same way I did. Start with a 90-second timer. Then move it to three minutes. Then five. Then 10 minutes. If you have to keep going with the timer, do it. There is no shame in using it for as long as you need to help build this habit. You may find it useful. You may find it annoying, in which case you may need to adapt and build your own checking/feedback mechanism.

That's fine.

The important thing is to remember to check back in so that you can catch yourself when you start rushing around again automatically—because you will. Accept that, and work with it. It will keep you from becoming frustrated down the road. Trust me on this.

When your timer sounds, here are a few questions to ask yourself:

"Is there tension in my body?"

"Am I holding my breath?"

"Am I talking to myself again about how I feel?"

"Am I moving slowly enough to hit my Seven Percent Slower target?"

Notice that at no time will you ask yourself how you FEEL or try to change how you FEEL. You only want to observe what you are doing, *not* how you're feeling. Your goal is to slow down, not to instantly banish your anxiety, fear, or stress. One goal at a time, please.

When you stop to check on these items, reset and slow down again if you need to. This is a learning process. You're not going to master going Seven Percent Slower in two days, so please don't expect that of yourself.

Things You Can Practice That Will Help You Go Seven Percent Slower

I've already talked about the need to practice going slower as often as you can. I don't want to tell you that Seven Percent Slower is some mystical lifestyle change, but you should also not think of this as an "on-demand" trick you only use when feeling amped up. It just doesn't work that way and won't work for you if you do this. When you practice a new habit, you get better at it. When you practice going slower as often as you can, slowing down by this little bit (seven percent really isn't much) will automatically become part of your life.

So … practice! Practice your new slowness whenever you can and whenever you think about it. Beyond moving more slowly, you can practice some specific things daily to help you accomplish your Seven Percent Slower mission.

If you know my work in general, what I am about to tell you is going to sound VERY familiar to you. At the risk of sounding like a broken record, here are some skills you should make time for every day. You don't need a lot of time. Just 15 minutes in the morning or evening will make a difference.

There are also resources for these skills and practices on my website at theanxioustruth.com/skills. I urge you to take advantage of them, at least as a starting point.

Muscle relaxation. Learning progressive muscle relaxation (PMR) will teach you how to recognize the feeling of tension in your body and how to recognize what letting it go feels like. It only takes a few minutes to run through a PMR exercise. Not only that, but it's a worthwhile investment of time.

Diaphragmatic breathing. Again, this is a skill that only takes a few minutes to practice each day. Learning to breathe into your belly with regular cadence is a wonderful adjunct to slowing things down. It's not difficult to understand, but especially if you are a chronic breath holder or over-breather, it may take some time to get good at. Take that time.

Focus. Part of building the foundation for this slowdown is honing the ability to put your attention where you want it and keeping it there. This is the skill of focus training, which is part and parcel of basic meditation. Earlier I wrote that Seven Percent Slower is not about becoming some kind of new-age yogi shaman, but that meditation and mindfulness were certainly related to the concept. I firmly believe that practicing basic meditation for 5-10 minutes every day goes a long way toward building your ability to slow things down when you want or need to. There are benefits beyond this, of course, but for the purposes of this book, we will use the Seven Percent Slower goal as your introduction to meditation.

You can practice basic meditation using a simple focal point. It can be your breath, a visual point in space, an object you hold in your hand, or even the sensations of your feet hitting the ground in a walking meditation. Teaching you meditation skills is beyond the scope of this book, but I do provide pre-recorded meditations at no charge on the Insight Timer app (find me at theanxioustruth.com/insight) if you are interested in giving it a try. You can also use basic guided breath/focus meditation on my website at theanxioustruth.com/skills.

A Word About Things You CAN'T Slow Down

Before we end this chapter, let's take a moment to review the things over which you have no control. In reality, much of life is out of our control. That's just how life is. Sometimes we forget that, especially when we have a shiny new toy like Seven Percent Slower, and we want to bring it everywhere with us.

In my general work with anxiety, I am often asked by formerly anxious people if they can use "my method" (it's not a special method, and I didn't invent it) in other areas of life. They ask how they can float and accept through loss and grief, messy divorces, financial and legal troubles, pet problems, and myriad other life situations. I have to tell them that not everything is floating and accepting problems because not everything is.

The same holds true for Seven Percent Slower, which is just a subset of my anxiety teaching. Not everything in life can be controlled and slowed down.

Do not fall into the trap of seeing Seven Percent Slower as a panacea that will make everything better. Moving more slowly and mindfully through life does tend to make for a better life, but there are many situations in which going slower is not a primary coping or solving mechanism.

Here is a short list of things you can't slow down. Please don't try. You'll just wind up frustrated.

1. Your heartbeat.

Yes, you can influence your heart rate. Clearly, you can run down the street to speed it up and sit quietly to slow it down. This is true. But in the context of stress, anxiety, and fear, your heart rate can be largely out of your control. You may hate that your heart beats more quickly when you are anxious or stressed, but that is merely your body working as designed. When a threat is detected, correctly or not, your fear center is in charge. Your lizard brain gets to decide how fast your heart should beat. Trying to slow down your heart will frustrate you. If you want to feel like you are doing something about it, you can send safety signals to your lizard brain repeatedly to teach it that it doesn't need to jack up your heartbeat randomly every day.

2. Your thoughts.

Remember the part where I talked about how going inward and thinking excessively isn't helpful? I stand by my statement, but we also must acknowledge that humans *are* thinking machines. We think. It's what we do. Seven Percent Slower is not about stopping your thoughts or turning off your brain. Not in any way. Please do not try to do that. It will be very frustrating for you. You cannot slow or stop your thoughts on demand. What you can do is work on responding to them differently to teach Mr. Lizard Brain that your brain does not need to be in overdrive to remain safe.

3. The speed of others around you.

While you are trying to slow down, the world may be operating at high speeds around you. Others may be rushing. This is OK and largely out of your control. You are not the only anxious or stressed person on the planet. When you see others rushing around like George Costanza trying to look busy at work (extra points if you get the *Seinfeld* reference), understand that this is a choice *they* are making. You cannot slow them down, even though they may make you feel more anxious or stressed by rushing the way they are. You have to accept that they are free to do what they want to do and turn your focus on what YOU can do.

4. Anything outside your own skin.

This really isn't specific to the concept of Seven Percent Slower, but it is always helpful to acknowledge our lack of control when it comes to the Universe at large. We can rarely control or influence anything outside our skins or beyond our families or social circles. That's life. One of the things that drive us to need books like this one in the first place is trying to control what we are *unable* to control. I don't want to get on a rant about this, but there is tremendous freedom and power in accepting just how much of life is beyond our control and working within that framework.

When we accept that which we cannot control,
we master that which we can.

Now let's look at the benefits of going Seven Percent Slower.

Chapter 10 — The Benefits of Going Seven Percent Slower

This chapter could be a book by itself. I'll do my best to keep it brief and focus on the anxiety and stress-related benefits of going Seven Percent Slower. But the benefits go way beyond that.

We've seen how slowing things down as part of your overall anxiety and stress improvement strategy isn't easy and automatic. You have old habits to identify and new habits to build. You have to practice tasks and be repetitive and consistent in your effort. Not only that, but you must be willing to make mistakes, catch those mistakes, and fix those mistakes. This isn't rocket science, but it also isn't a walk in the park.

So, why go through it?

Here are just a few good reasons for you, in no particular order.

1. Lower overall nervous energy level.

We love energy. We hate nervous energy. Nervous energy isn't productive. It's quite counterproductive when you get down to brass tacks. When your days are spent amped up and full of nervous energy due to anxiety, fear, and stress, anything we can do to bring that down is going to be beneficial. Remember, we are never trying to banish the anxiety, fear, and stress response from our lives. That's not a realistic goal. We can, however, work to slowly reduce that non-productive, disruptive, distracting nervous energy. It doesn't mean instant Zen, but it will help keep you from spiraling out of control, as you may often do now.

2. Increased feeling of control, competence, and confidence over time.

When you are being ruled most of the time by your overactive and overworked lizard brain, you may start to feel out of control and largely powerless over almost everything. The process of learning to slow down means you get some control back. More accurately, you learn to realize and use the control you've always had. When you work to change your automatic rushing response to anxiety, fear, and stress, you regain a sense of competence and confidence. You will see through repeated experiences that you CAN make different choices about how you respond when your lizard brain makes demands. When that happens, you can't help but feel more in control and capable of handling what previously felt overwhelming to you.

3. **Turning down the fear/stress/anxiety response. Tuning it back into reality.**

You've learned that trying to turn OFF your lizard brain—your threat detection and response system—is not possible or desirable. But while we are not working to turn off that natural system, we can turn it DOWN. Think of your overactive threat detection and response system as a loudspeaker with a volume knob and no power switch. Learning to go Seven Percent Slower helps turn down the volume even when you can't turn off the power. Your lizard brain might constantly be screaming at the top of its lungs at you, but when we slow things down, we help to slowly turn down that volume control.

When we stick with this plan and work at it, we can make giant strides toward teaching Mr. Lizard Brain to use his indoor voice again, and only when needed. That's a big deal. It changes everything.

4. **Greater "distress tolerance" skills.**

Anxiety, fear, stress, and the response that comes with them are definitely distressing. Feeling overwhelmed, powerless, and out of control is distressing. Feeling like your body is working against you is distressing. The whole affair is a big ball of distress! A non-productive response to anxiety, fear, and stress is often based on an underlying belief that no distress is permissible or tolerable and that all distress must be avoided at all costs. Nobody likes to feel bad, but the fact of the matter is that humans sometimes do. We get no guarantee of days filled with bliss and smooth sailing. Occasionally, the road is bumpy, and we feel emotions we want to avoid. Throwing up your hands and declaring little pitfalls a disaster because you have adopted a zero-distress tolerance policy is not helpful in any way and leads to the place you are in now.

Learning to slow down when anxiety, fear, and stress are triggering a demand for speed will help you build a greater tolerance for this distress. Slowing down and navigating thoughtfully and purposefully through high-anxiety or high-stress situations teaches you that you are capable of handling more than you give yourself credit for. Your tolerance for distress rises. Given that distress is a fact of life, no matter how much you wish it wasn't, increasing your "distress tolerance" skill set is no small matter. Get better at tolerating distress when it rears its head, and you will essentially get better at life. That's never bad.

Let me clarify one thing here. I am not saying that you will learn to passively accept crap when life throws it at you. You are not here to learn how to sit still and let life beat you about the neck and shoulders. You are simply learning that you are not powerless in those moments, that you can tolerate periods of distress, and that you are in control and competent even when you've always believed otherwise. Learning to go Seven Percent Slower helps take the bite off those distressing feelings and situations. It makes them seem much more manageable.

5. Improved crisis navigation skills.

Elite athletes often speak of seeing events unfold in front of them in slow motion. While everyone around them is frantic, the best of the best seems to move fluidly and effortlessly through high-pressure situations. They exhibit a calmness amidst the chaos. This enables them to score that big goal, make a key defensive play, or perform some other heroic action that saves the day or wins the game when a victory is implausible.

One of the common phrases in our lexicon, used to describe that person that you want by your side in an emergency, is "cool under pressure." We've all heard it, and we all know that person. The building is burning, and they are unfazed, calmly doing what needs to be done to put out the fire or get everyone to safety.

Here's news: learning to slow things down when under duress (i.e., anxious, afraid, or stressed-out) is a part of becoming this sort of person! Still, you need to know that the calm, collected, go-to person may look cooler than the other side of the pillow, but they feel things, too. They're afraid. They feel stress. They understand the gravity of a situation when it goes sideways. The difference is that they have learned they can mute that lizard brain response and not let themselves get out of control. They can respond with appropriate action rather than disordered avoidance or frantic escape.

When you learn to go Seven Percent Slower, you can become that person. You may not entirely change who you are, nor should you, but improving your performance in a crisis—is a major benefit that should not be overlooked.

6. Lower threat distortion/magnification level.

Your overworked and over-tired lizard brain does not know if it needs to sh-t or wind its watch at any given moment. Your threat detection mechanism is firing loudly when it shouldn't with an extreme level of distortion. Does it feel like everything is a disaster? Like life is one nightmare after the next? When you read that, do you honestly think this is an accurate assessment of reality or the result of distorted misfiring from your fear center?

Anxious, highly stressed people feel like they live in a pressure cooker all the time. But it does not have to be that way because, by and large, it is not that way. Of course, there are challenges and stressors in life, but when your nerves are raw, and you are sensitive to everything, even the smallest problem gets blown up into a life-altering international incident.

Remember how going Seven Percent Slower sends "all clear" signals back down to your lizard brain? Remember how over time, those signals teach your fear center that it can take regular breaks? When your fear center dials itself back and slows down along with you, that magnification and distortion also get dialed back. What seems like a nightmare now doesn't seem quite so bad when you've helped Mr. Lizard Brain chill out a bit. The distortion and magnification creating that pressure cooker feeling start to fade away, and life gets more manageable for you.

7. **Greater alignment with value-driven choices rather than fear-driven choices.**

You may have heard about living a "value-driven life." This is a popular concept in self-help and self-development. It might sound all spiritual and new-agey, but it's not. Living a value-driven life means making decisions and choices based on what matters to you rather than fear and avoidance. When you're living in a near panic all the time, rushing around and taking orders from a misfiring fear center, your values often do not enter into your decisions. You want to make good life choices that keep you connected to what you love and care about, but you mostly find yourself just surviving day-to-day. Fear is calling the shots, and escape and avoidance are your primary strategies, even when you don't want them to be.

Learning to slow things down—maybe seven percent—plays a key role in re-balancing your decision-making process. When you turn down the volume of your fear center, your values can re-enter the picture. You can make choices and decisions more purposefully, with a clearer mind. You will stop making all your decisions based on fear. You will start making decisions based on what truly matters to you. Learning to go Seven Percent Slower helps move you closer to living a desired value-driven life.

8. **Improved analytical ability. Moving more slowly leads to thinking more clearly.**

"Change your thoughts, change your life!" No. It doesn't work that way. If you want to change your life, start by changing your life. Behaviorally. Change what you do, and you can change what you think. More importantly, when you change what you do, you can change HOW you think. Overly anxious, overly stressed people will often say they can't think straight. Everything feels like too much. They make fear-based decisions with very little analysis or thought beyond them. If you are here, too, everything is reflexive, automatic, and driven by the primitive parts of your brain. Clarity seems a million miles away and unreachable much of the time.

Chapter 1 of this book asserts that your brain needs a few days off. When you learn to go Seven Percent Slower, you bank vacation time for your brain. or at least the parts tasked with threat detection and response. These are the parts that matter most in this context. When your fear center takes days off, clarity returns. You find yourself thinking clearly. The analytical part of your brain finally gets some breathing room and can participate in your decision-making process again.

One of the most amazing things I hear daily from anxious people who do this work and see improvement is that they've realized they've been thinking so much, but not clearly, and not getting anywhere. Suddenly, after undertaking specific tasks designed to address their panic and anxiety, they find themselves thinking LESS, but more clearly. What they need to do gets done again as a result. You may have never seen the relief in the eyes of another human when they discover that they are not mentally broken. I have the privilege of seeing that look every day. It's quite remarkable. Learning to go Seven Percent Slower is a step in that direction. Maybe one day I'll get to see that look in your eyes, too.

I could go on and on when it comes to the direct and secondary benefits of learning to simply SLOW DOWN. But this is not supposed to be a giant 400-page tome (I already wrote one of those), so I'll end the list here.

Hopefully, you get the idea.

Learning to go Seven Percent Slower comes with benefits, and they are many.

Chapter 11 — "So I'm never allowed to go fast?"

You may be wondering if you are never allowed to move quickly again.

It's a fair question to ask. And it's an important enough question that deserves its own chapter—even if it's a short one.

If you are someone who has always worn your speed demonness as a badge of honor (be honest), then this question is particularly important to you, isn't it?

"I'm the fast guy!"

"I'm the fast thinker!"

"I'm the one who gets there first!"

I see you.

You think that rushing through life, jamming as much as possible into every minute, is good. You see yourself in some ways as superior because you are fast. It is not my intention to imply that you are an egotistical lunatic. We all have traits we associate with ourselves that we hold on to, like hot death, because they reinforce our belief in who we hope to be. Many people identify themselves with speed. I was that person once. I thought thinking faster and getting done faster than everyone else in the room was a sign of achievement or inherent excellence. That's why learning to slow down was a challenge for me and even prompted me to come up with the whole Seven Percent Slower idea during my anxiety recovery. I did not want to accept that speed was part of my problem, but it was.

At this point, you may be thinking that I am asking you to give up part of your identity by learning to slow down, but that is not the case. Speed does not have to be totally banished from your life. It just needs to be used more purposefully and for the right reasons.

Spoiler alert: ego and self-image
are not the right reasons.

Sometimes life requires speed. Speed is not inherently evil. Context REALLY matters. In this book, we are concerned with the context of your reaction to anxiety, fear, and stress. While I just spent an entire chapter singing the praises of going slower and how those benefits spill into the rest of your life, I must acknowledge that sometimes speed is required and helpful.

Speed is required and helpful when responding to an actual, real, current physical threat, for instance.

*How many Zen masters have been eaten by charging
lions over the years? We may never know, but I bet it's
at least one, and that dude should have recognized
that sometimes you do need to panic.*

You live, you learn, you get eaten by a lion. Sh-t happens.

We live in a world where there are deadlines. This is a fact, unpleasant though it may be. Speed helps us meet deadlines now and then. Having to work quickly sometimes creates increased focus and can even spark creativity. The popular YouTuber musician Adam Neely shared an excellent video where he collaborated with a fellow YouTuber to write an entire original album in 24 hours. The most interesting thing about Adam's experiment was seeing how not having the luxury of overthinking and overanalyzing helped him remain open to all the new musical ideas that popped up in his head. He needed them to flow freely, and the speed with which he was forced to work unlocked that. You may fully understand this because you may have experienced this for yourself from time to time. I know I have.

Occasionally, we just need to FEEL faster. There. I said it. In a book dedicated to going slower, I agree that sometimes feeling like we are moving at a high speed is what we need. Every so often, we need to feel faster than the next guy because we *just do.* Other times we need to feel faster to help wiggle us out of low points or ruts where we may be stuck. Sometimes we need to feel faster as a celebration of accomplishment or as an acknowledgment of being alive.

Speed is not always evil.

Sometimes speed makes us feel good on a mental or emotional level. This is OK. Don't let anyone tell you that your entire life must be lived in slow motion. Enjoying the feeling of speed or even rushing sometimes does not make you an un-enlightened loser. It makes you human.

Humans are designed to experience many situations, environments, and emotions. Being fully human means that sometimes (not always, please) you will rush through life like a strung-out mongoose, and that will have to do.

The key to success within the context of Seven Percent Slower is learning when it is appropriate to speed up and when it is appropriate to slow down. During periods of anxiety, fear, and stress without the presence of real and present danger, slowing down is appropriate. When speed is pouring fuel on your anxiety or stress fire, slowing down is appropriate. When you feel out of control or overwhelmed, slowing down is appropriate. But this does not mean that you are never allowed to go fast EVER again.

Sometimes, speed is good. Work on recognizing when this is the case and when it is not. Learning to go Seven Percent Slower is part of a better overall strategy for addressing your anxiety and stress issues. When you improve your relationship with and reaction to anxiety and stress, you'll naturally get better at seeing context. You'll get better at knowing when to slow down, when to speed up, and when it doesn't matter either way. Learning to go Seven Percent Slower is one step toward getting better at "reading the room" when it comes to the need for speed.

So yes, you can still go fast sometimes when you need or want to. The world won't end if you do.

I told you this was going to be a short chapter.

Chapter 12 — Beyond Seven Percent Slower

What lies beyond the Seven Percent?

Seven Percent Slower was conceived as a mental device years ago during the hardest part of my recovery from my anxiety disorders. It was something I came up with to help me remember to slow down when I needed to slow down. It was a tool for me.

Think of it as an action trigger. Seven Percent Slower is not so much a method or philosophy as it is a way to connect you to a larger method and larger philosophies. I have not built my life upon going Seven Percent Slower, but I have certainly incorporated it into my life well beyond my anxiety recovery journey.

When I hit a wall, I slow down for a bit.

When I start to feel like I may have bitten off more than I can chew, I slow down.

When confronted with major decisions, I slow down before I make them, which helps me make them from a place of greater mental clarity in accordance with my values rather than my stress level.

When the people around me are frantic and reacting poorly to a given situation, I can slow down, and it helps bring order and direction where needed.

When I feel strong emotions like anger or sadness, I can feel them fully, but I can also slow down, so I don't act upon them hastily. Learning to slow down when appropriate helps me honor my emotions without being ruled by them all the time.

I could write another few thousand words about all the ways that Seven Percent Slower lives on in my life and likely will in yours. The point is that alone, going slower is not going to change your life in a miraculous way. If I can tell you anything at this stage, it would be to remember that there is no one "magic bullet" that fixes all your anxiety, fear, and stress problems. Seven Percent Slower is not a cure for what ails you. It's a stepping stone toward finding all the tools that can work together to achieve your goal.

I have written so many words in the last five years on the topic of anxiety and fear, and I cannot count the number of times I've used words like "acceptance," "surrender," and "courage."

Now, I spend a large portion of my life teaching people why going toward what they fear is the way past that fear. I write and often speak about concepts, methods, and paradigms that are inherently counterintuitive and feel like the opposite of what anxious and stressed-out people want to do.

There is resistance. Large, overflowing buckets of resistance. In this thing that I do, I am continually swimming in a current of nothing but resistance. People want to feel good. They want to feel better. They want to solve their anxiety and stress problems. But people also don't want to do scary or difficult things. I do not blame them, and if you want to avoid doing scary or difficult things, I do not blame you either. This is how humans are wired. We seek comfort. We avoid discomfort.

Unfortunately, and at the risk of sounding like some kind of life-coaching cliché monster, there are valuable lessons to be learned in the uncomfortable places.

The personal development space online generally makes me want to gag because half of what we see there never makes it past mindless platitudes and low-hanging clickbait fruit, but there is truth beneath much of it.

Good things happen in tight spaces. Gold is forged in the fires of discomfort and distress sometimes. That is the truth beneath the torrent of inspirational memes.

Most times, we are unwilling to dig for that truth and experience and live it. Like I said, we are creatures designed to take the path of least resistance, and it shows. Everyone wants to get better, but everyone also wants it to happen without working for it. Really working for it.

Enough ranting. Let me bring it back to Seven Percent Slower.

Learning to go Seven Percent Slower is difficult. It is also a resistance breaker. It is the switch that can often turn on that light bulb you've been hoping to switch on for months. Or years. When we learn to slow down in a practical, easy-to-grasp way, often we find that it gives us the little push we need to fully embrace what we know in our bones will be the path to a better life. We've been resisting because that path isn't paved as smoothly as we hoped it would be, but when we slow down, we often shed our resistance.

You may be familiar with my podcast, *The Anxious Truth*, my other books, *The Anxious Truth*, and *An Anxiety Story*, or what I regularly say on social media. If so, then you may be in that place where you desperately want to start overcoming your anxiety problems, but you just can't seem to get the need to do all the scary stuff I talk about to "click."

I feel you.

I see you.

Slow down.

That's a good place to start. When you stop trying to think your way into embracing anxiety recovery and start behaving your way into that embrace by simply slowing down, what you are struggling with can change.

If you are living immersed in stress all day long and trying to find some way to solve your problems that seem insurmountable, I see you, too. Life is full of hard problems that require difficult actions to address. Life forces us into the uncomfortable places no matter what we do to try to stop it from happening. If you spend your days rushing around, huffing and puffing, lamenting your misfortune, and shirking your problems … slow down. Learning to slow down is a reasonable first step toward becoming "ready" to face your challenges. You can't solve them all at once, and you can't change direction all at once, but you can make that first move. Learning to go Seven Percent Slower can be your first move.

I hope that I have given you a way to "pump the brakes." If this book has given you a tool that helps create a little space for you to maneuver in, then it has been worth the effort to write. I believe that you should take the time and make the effort to understand the concept of Seven Percent Slower and then practice actually slowing yourself down when needed. I believe in my heart that it will make a difference in your life immediately and down the road in other areas.

I am confident that the simple act of learning to recognize your rushing habit, understanding what drives it, and working to change it, can open the door to wider and deeper progress when it comes to handling anxiety, stress, and fear.

I can't be 100 percent sure of this because we can never be that sure of anything in life.

But I am at least Seven Percent surer, and that's something. ;-)

Those Resources
(One. More. Time!)

My Website:
https://theanxioustruth.com

The Anxious Truth Podcast:
https://theanxioustruth.com/listen

The Anxious Truth: A Step-By-Step Guide to Understanding and Overcoming Anxiety, Panic, and Agoraphobia:
https://theanxioustruth.com/recoveryguide

An Anxiety Story: How I Overcame, Panic, Anxiety, and Agoraphobia
https://theanxioustruth.com/mystory

The Anxious Truth on Instagram:
https://theanxioustruth.com/instagram

The Anxious Truth on Facebook:
https://theanxioustruth.com/facebook

The Anxious Truth on YouTube:
https://theanxioustruth.com/youtube

The Anxious Truth on Twitter:
https://theanxioustruth.com/twitter

About The Author

Drew Linsalata is the creator and host of *The Anxious Truth*, a slightly unorthodox anxiety-related podcast that's been in full swing since 2014. With over two million downloads (and growing), *The Anxious Truth* has spawned a large, vibrant and engaged social media community of amazing humans supporting, inspiring, encouraging and empowering each other to overcome anxiety and fear.

Having suffered with anxiety, panic disorder, agoraphobia, and depression several times over a 20-year period, Drew got it together once and for all in 2008. Since then, life has been happy, productive, and "normal" (although we'd all be hard-pressed to define normal at times).

For the last 15 years, Drew has been active in the online anxiety community, working to use his experience and understanding to help those traveling the path he's traveled. His no-nonsense approach to these problems and willingness to provide direct, actionable advice even when it might not be easy to hear has established him as a unique voice in the community.

In 2020, Drew published two Amazon bestselling books on anxiety and anxiety recovery. *An Anxiety Story* and *The Anxious Truth* have quickly become required reading for anyone suffering with anxiety and in need of education, instruction, inspiration, encouragement and empowerment.

Disclaimer

I am not a doctor or a trained mental health therapist. Seven Percent Slower is based on my experience and the shared experiences of thousands that I have had the privilege of inter- acting with over many years. Seven Percent Slower should not be construed as diagnosis, therapy, or treatment. Seven Percent Slower is not medical advice and should not be used as such. I always advocate for educating oneself and making use of tools like this book alongside expert mental and physical health treatment provided by trained, licensed professionals. Self-help is a wonderful thing, but when needed, always consult with a trained professional.

Made in United States
North Haven, CT
08 April 2024

51077630R00075